Make it a
HABIT!

Make it a
HABIT!
Creating Health and Happiness
for your Body, Mind, and Spirit

Sylvie Heyman, RN, MPS, DC, LAc

Dedication

To my husband, David,
my rock, who made it all possible.

Acknowledgments

It takes a village not just to raise a child but also to write and publish a book.

I am grateful to many people who supported me through this journey. I thank my husband David for encouraging me to step out of my comfort zone and follow a passion that was dormant in me for many years. I am indebted to all the patients and clients I have helped throughout the years who provided the background for the stories I have written.

I am immensely grateful to my editor, Susan Suffes, for her guidance and support every step of the way. Her insightful feedback helped me convey my thoughts and experiences, polishing and shaping my manuscript into a real book.

I want to thank three authors: Charles Duhigg, whose book *The Power of Habits* sparkled my fascination for the topic of Habits; Dr. Wayne Scott Andersen, for his teachings on the true meaning of health coaching; and my friend, Natalie Bober, distinguished author of 12 biographies as well as children's books and a memoir, whose passion for writing inspired me and awakened my own latent fervor for writing this book.

I also want to express my gratitude to Outskirts Press for accepting my manuscript for publication. I specifically thank Catherine Tidd for her words of encouragement and Bridget Horstmann, my author Representative, for her patience through all the changes I imposed on her on an almost daily basis.

Lastly, I thank my family and friends who were interested in my work and followed my progress throughout my journey.

Table of Contents

Introduction: The Body, Mind and Spirit of Habits i

Chapter One: Change Your Habits, Change Your Life 1

Chapter Two: The Neuroscience and Psychology of Habits ... 11

Chapter Three: Many Habits, Many Methods 41

Chapter Four: The Triple A's of Body, Mind, and Spirit 61

Chapter Five: The Habits of Health 89

Chapter Six: The Habit of Healthy Eating and
                Reaching a Healthy Weight 105

Chapter Seven: Habits of the Spirit 129

Chapter Eight: Habits for Children 135

Final Words 153

Sources 155

I Am A Habit

I am your constant companion.
I am your greatest helper or your heaviest burden.
I will push you onward or drag you down to failure.
I am completely at your command.

Half the things you do, you might just as well turn over to me.
and I will be able to do them quickly and correctly.
I am easily managed; you must merely be firm with me.
Show me exactly how you want something done, and after
    a few lessons I will do it autmatically.
I am the servant of all great men.
And, alas, of all failures as well.
Those who are great, I have made great.
Those who are failures, I have made failures.

I am not a machine, though I work with all the precision
    of a machine.
Plus, the intelligence of a man.
You may run me for profit, or for ruin; it makes no differ-
    ence to me.

Take me, train me, be firm with me and I will put the world
   at your feet.
Be easy with me and I will destroy you.
Who am I?
I am HABIT !

–Anonymous

INTRODUCTION:

The Body, Mind and Spirit of Habits

Elie Wiesel said: "If I survived, it must be for some reason. I must do something with my life ... because in my place, someone else could have been saved."

His words express exactly the way I felt as a child and still do. I believe that there is a force in the universe that guides my life and all I have to do is listen carefully for the messages that are sent to me.

Why didn't I end up like Anne Frank? She was in Holland while I lived in Belgium, the country next door. Why was I able to leave Europe in 1940, after one year of escaping through France and Spain and landing in Portugal, where a man by the name of Aristides De Sousa Mendes saved my life and my family?

As the Portuguese consul-general in Bordeaux, France, Mr. Mendes saved the lives of thousands of refugees fleeing Nazi Germany. He locked himself up in his office for three days, not to be disturbed, so he could stamp one visa after another. We left Portugal and arrived in Brazil on November 28, 1940. Then I contracted diphtheria. As much as I needed to be in a hospital for my grave condition, the doctor told my parents that if I went to the hospital it would be to die. He gave me a serum and told my parents to pray. The doctor who saved my life was a German and he was not Jewish. It was another message that I was to live for a reason and believe in the good of people.

A few years later we settled in Argentina, where my father had brothers who were smart enough to leave Europe a few years before Hitler's invasion. Still, it wasn't easy to live under the dictatorship of Juan Peron. We had to be very careful not to attract the attention of the police, but nonetheless we were grateful to be alive and free.

Growing up under these circumstances it became clear to me, early on, that I was spared for a reason. When I played games with my friends or by myself, I liked the role of the doctor or nurse. It wasn't long before I realized what my calling would be: It would be to help people live healthy lives.

MY PATH TO UNDERSTANDING HABITS

My first profession in the healing arts was nursing. For 26 years I worked as a Registered Nurse. I specialized in obstetrical nursing and later on worked as a cardiac operating room supervisor and instructor. When it was time to switch from high tech to high touch I went to chiropractic college. Loving this philosophy of healing, I went on to study acupuncture and practiced both professions for 24 and 18 years respectively. When I was contemplating retirement I decided instead to move on and continue to pursue new ways of helping people find better health in their lives by taking on a different approach, that of a health coach.

It was as a health coach that I recognized how much the role of habits plays in every aspect of our lives: 40 to 45 percent of our daily actions are based on habits.

I was preparing for a series of workshops on healthy habits when my research led me to several habit formation and change methods developed by other authors who were obviously just as smitten as I was about the topic. I was particularly inspired by Charles Duhigg's *The Power of Habits*.

There seemed to be a common thread in all the methods that I reviewed: They stressed the importance of starting with little baby steps that would become keystone habits and promote other habits to emerge. There were

studies about triggers, routines, rewards and the importance of repetition. There were also theories on readiness
for change, as well as different personality traits that would
make people more or less inclined to succeed with different methods. They all seemed right on target.

The more I read about habits the more I thought about
the thousands of patients I'd treated over the years who
would have benefited from learning more about methods
for creating new habits or change their bad ones.

Looking back on my experiences as a Registered Nurse,
a Chiropractor, an Acupuncturist, and now a health coach,
I believe that most of the health issues that we face in our
nation, and the world at large, are a result of poor habits.
We spend so much time trying to fix what's wrong and
educate the public to healthy lifestyles—i.e. learning about
healthy food choices, stressing the importance of exercise,
good sleep, and stress reduction—that we often neglect
how to help people create new habits or change the bad
ones. This is a field of its own that requires understanding
human nature, patience to work through habits that are
deeply ingrained in everyday behavior, and knowledge of
various habit forming/changing techniques.

Because there is a global obesity epidemic, and I am
a healthcare practitioner, many of the examples cited in
this book revolve around habits of disease. However, the
basic principles and methods outlined in this book can

be used for all different kinds of habits of the body, mind, and spirit.

There is one overarching message that I wish to convey in this book: habits affect our world to an enormous extent, one person at a time. For me, the essence of habits takes on a holistic view that encompasses the body, mind, and spirit of a human being.

CHAPTER ONE:

Change Your Habits, Change Your Life

The rumor, that something strange had been removed from a patient's stomach, spread like a forest fire. I ran to Operating Room 5 to see what the buzz was all about. There it was, a little larger than a grapefruit, on a steel table. "What is it ?" I asked the small crowd who pressed their noses close to the glass window. "It's a hairball," someone answered. Later, at a staff meeting, the story of 16 year-old Juliette was revealed. She had a history of twirling her long hair with her fingers and chewing the ends. When her doctor asked her why she did that, she said, "I don't know. It's just a habit I guess."

In all the years that I've practiced nursing, chiropractic, and acupuncture I was well aware that many of my patients were victims of unhealthy habits. Clearly, nail biting or chewing cuticles are habits more common than eating hair, but let's not kid ourselves. There are many habits that can bring about serious health issues just as eating hair did for Juliette. Everybody knows by now that smoking is linked to lung cancer, and poor eating habits and obesity are associated with heart disease, high blood pressure, Type 2 diabetes, some forms of cancers, and numerous musculoskeletal conditions that often end up with hip and knee replacement.

As a Registered Nurse working in surgery, I saw count-less patients who could not be cleared for surgery because of their obesity. Those who did have surgery suffered a myriad of complications plus they required more anesthesia and additional medications. They experienced more postoperative pain and were at greater risk of infection and cardiovascular collapse. As an Obstetrical Nurse, I saw the correlation between obesity and gestational diabetes, and that when women required a C-section they often suffered the same complication risks of obese patients. As a Chiropractor, I saw a huge difference in patients' progress in their low back and knee pain once they lost their excess weight. As an Acupuncturist, I treated numerous conditions related to obesity such as high blood pressure, sleep apnea, and hormonal dysfunction. In all my healthcare careers my goal was to teach my patients the importance of a healthy lifestyle.

Many of my patients needed to lose weight, exercise, get quality sleep and decrease stress in their lives. I helped a lot of people in my professional life but what I noticed was that unless they changed their habits most of them needed to be treated for longer periods of time. Also, many of them returned for treatment for the same conditions again and again. I wanted to help more people lose weight and learn the habits of health for long-term success. But my training did not prepare me to deal with these goals, and it certainly didn't give me the necessary tools to focus on helping them change those habits.

In order to use those specific tools, I embarked on a study to learn all I could about the art of coaching. I continued my training and earned my Certification as a Nutrition and Wellness Consultant from the American Fitness Professional Associates (AFPA). The National Academy of Sports Medicine (NASM) also certified me as a Fitness Instructor. Armed with this new body of knowledge, I could offer my patients a structured eating plan, guide them through their health journey and oversee their progress. Consequently, I have helped hundreds of people reach their ideal weight and adopt a lifestyle that included a healthy body, mind, and spirit.

Changing habits is something I personally understand very well.

MY FIRSTHAND EXPERIENCE

When I was 14 years old my family and I immigrated to the USA from Argentina, This kind of upheaval is difficult at any age, and it's especially hard for a teenager. For the first two years I cried myself to sleep. That's when I started to pick the skin on the index and middle finger of my left hand until they bled. Not only that; I picked the skin of my heels as well. Sometimes I could hardly walk from the pain I inflicted upon myself. The habit was almost unconscious and I did it while studying, reading, before going to sleep, when baby sitting, watching TV, and particularly when I longed for my friends and the life that I had left behind. Why would I want to mutilate myself that way? Perhaps the physical pain I inflicted on myself was a way of diverting my attention away from the emotional void I felt.

In my case, a change of environment triggered the development of a new habit that started from loneliness and homesickness. After I gradually began to make friends and became more accustomed to surroundings I stopped crying and was happier. Still, the habit continued, and off and on I picked my fingers, sometimes just because I liked the "sting" it gave me.

I learned early on how difficult it could be to break certain habits, especially those with a strong emotional attachment. I also learned that changing habits is not a linear process. I've had some setbacks over the years but I keep my awareness and I am in tune with my emotions, knowing that my habit could return with full vengeance if I don't keep a check on it. Today it only surfaces occasionally when I am very stressed or bored. My own experience with this destructive habit has made me more compassionate about helping others get rid of their habits.

Many years later, my experiences helped me to understand why older people become so "set" in their ways. My mother hesitated for two years to move from her apartment into a retirement home. In her early nineties, she needed a little help in her everyday activities such as food shopping, cooking and cleaning. She was also lonely because so many of her friends had died. Because she lived in Florida and we lived in New York, I suggested she relocate to a place close to us. She refused most vehemently. I couldn't understand why she wouldn't want to be closer to her only daughter and her grandsons and their families. We kept visiting various places in Florida with her and she always found something she didn't like about them. We thought she was stubborn and argued with her all too often.

It wasn't until I delved into the study of habits that I understood her feelings. She didn't want to give up her habits; they made her feel secure, as did the familiarity of her environment. It took a lot of prodding and patience and eventually she entertained the idea. She found a place where a few acquaintances were living. Yes, her environment did change and as much as possible she hung on to her old habits until she gradually became comfortable and happy in her new lifestyle.

Habits are an important part of our lives and the longer we live the more ingrained they become. Making changes in our senior years is a defining moment in life when we need to let go of that which is comfortable and a part of us. Adults should be sensitive to the needs of their elder parents and give them the dignity of choosing which habits they are willing to give up.

HABITS ON A CONTINUUM

It is not always obvious how and why habits begin, but we do know that many of our habits begin in childhood. The dual nature of habits exists on a continuum, with the good ones (such as brushing our teeth in the morning) on one end, to the bad ones (binge eating) and the pathological (addictions, compulsive behaviors) on the other end of the spectrum. Whether they are good, bad, or pathological, they are all born through the same neurological pathways. Habits emerge through associative learning that arises from a response to a cue, a trigger. They become fully integrated in our behavior by the act of repetition.

One would wonder why our brain is hard-wired to create habits. What purpose do they serve? When are they beneficial and when do they become pathological? Why are they so pervasive in our personal lives, in sports, businesses, organizations and society at large? (You'll read more about the neuroscience of habits in Chapter Two.)

At the core of this phenomenon is the notion that habits allow the brain to quiet down so it can focus on other things. You're probably aware of many of them. For example, you can plan your presentation at the board meeting while parallel parking. You can think of what you want to wear when you're brushing your hair. You can mentally list your grocery needs while getting dressed.

FROM WORKSHOP TO HABITS

Initially, my work as a health coach focused on helping people reach their ideal weight and learning the habits of health for long-term success. My fascination about the subject of habits, in general, emerged from a workshop I presented at a cardiologist's office on the "5 Habits of Health for Reaching a Healthy Weight and Vibrant Life." The first part of my presentation focused on just habits: how and why they are formed and how the attendees could change the negative behaviors that were sabotaging their health.

From then on, I began to pay closer attention to what people were saying and noticed that the word habit would crop up frequently in personal as well as business conversations. I started researching the topic: where habits come from, why they dominate our lives and how to change them. My fascination grew. I always recognized the link between habits as a part of lifestyle and obesity, but now the scope of how habits affect our lives widened. If a person is stuck in a habit mode, such as snacking on cookies throughout the day, it is difficult to overcome the temptation without looking at changing that habit. If a person is stuck in the habit of procrastination it is just as difficult to do today what can be done tomorrow.

Awareness of how habits dominate so many aspects of our lives became a central focus in my mind.

JOHN'S JOURNEY

I had been treating John off and on for many years for chronic low back pain. He was one of the first patients I helped as a health coach. He was 80 pounds overweight, had been diagnosed with Type 2 diabetes and high blood pressure by his primary care physician, and relayed to me a family history of heart disease. He had gone on many of what he called 'successful' diets in the past but always gained his weight back. That wasn't surprising. According to Dr. Wayne Scott Andersen, a leading physician in the preventative arena of nutritional intervention and lifestyle management, "Eighty-five percent of people who go on a diet without behavioral support gain the weight back within two years. [1]

After John experienced his first bout of angina, he decided to follow the recommendation of his physician to see a cardiologist. The angiogram revealed a high-grade blockage, in a critical area, which was determined to be an indication for surgery. However, there was one big obstacle: he needed to lose weight first.

"Can you help me, Dr. Heyman?" he asked with desperation. He realized that he couldn't simply go on another diet. Instead, he needed to understand his eating habits. First I put him on a structured eating plan for weight loss. More importantly, he started a program that would help him change his poor habits to healthy ones. Six months later, with the necessary weight loss, he was cleared for bypass surgery. Today, John is at his healthiest weight since he graduated high school. He exercises daily, makes healthy eating choices, gets restful sleep and enjoys a satisfying life. "I'm not worried anymore that I'm going to drop dead any minute," he shared with me at his last visit to my office.

WHAT YOU WILL FIND OUT ABOUT HABITS

Habits, once formed, never go away. They are the outcome of old decisions, and they can be changed, but only through new decisions and choices.

In this book you'll read about various methodologies that have been created for that change to take place. Some techniques may suit certain situations better than others, and some people may be more attracted to a specific method. Others still may use a combination of various strategies that work best for them.

I hope that this book will assist health professionals in recognizing habits that get in the way of their patients' ability to heal and lead healthy lives. It is my fervent desire that it will also help parents establish a strong foundation for teaching healthy habits to their children.

You will read many stories about patients and clients who were held captive by their bad habits and came to use one or a combination of theories and practices that put them on the path to living a healthy life. It is my desire that you will find the right combination for yourself, and for those that you influence, to bring successful outcomes and transformations.

CHAPTER TWO:

The Neuroscience and Psychology of Habits

It never even occurred to me that I was a popcorn junkie until a time when I saw three movies in one week to catch up with the impending Academy Awards. With every movie I saw, I had to munch on popcorn. My feet automatically moved in the direction of the refreshment stand without one moment of hesitation. It didn't matter if I had just eaten lunch or if I was going to dinner after the movie. Hunger was seldom a trigger, although sometimes I'd 'save my appetite' to feed my habit. Strangely enough, I didn't even mind if the popcorn was stale when I ate it at the movies, but not otherwise. I discovered that when I bought popcorn at a festival and it was stale, I'd throw it out. "Hmmm," I remember saying to myself. "I wouldn't have minded it at the movies…"

I was totally immersed in my research about habits for a lecture when I came upon a study [2] that showed that people who eat popcorn every time they go to the movies—and if they ate it in the same manner, that is, picking up the popcorn with the same hand every time— are doing it out of habit. That was definitely me!

Similar studies indicated that just by switching hands, people consumed less popcorn. I tried that and definitely saw a difference in my popcorn habit. First I was eating less; instead of buying a tub I settled for small ones more often. In time, I gave up the habit altogether. Awareness and switching hands is all it took. What a wake-up call that was! Imagine having a habit and not even being aware of it? What if I had a habit that was seriously compromising my health and didn't know it?

This chapter is about how, where, and why habits are formed, along with the roles of willpower and motivation. Because it is so important to recognize our readiness to make any kind of change in our habits, I've included a model that describes the stages of readiness to make changes in one's life.

❧

HOW HABITS ARE WIRED

Although the study and research of the science of habit formation began in the early 1990's, it wasn't until the end of the 20th century that major advances in the field of cognitive behavioral psychology emerged globally. These developments offer a better understanding of the science of habit formation and its potential for change.

A clinical psychologist once told me that men and women are "wired" differently. "Certain areas of the brain light up differently in response to the same stimuli depending on the sex of the person," he explained. [3] Habits also light up in a different part of the brain when certain behaviors are acted out. The original thought or action, before it becomes a habit, starts in the prefrontal area of the brain, sometimes referred to as the higher brain. This is the part of the organ that deals with decision-making, social behavior, as well as planning complex cognitive behavior, and generally is responsible for orchestrating thoughts and actions.

Let me illustrate this point with my own personal experience. Several years ago I moved to Manhattan from the suburbs of Long Island. My entire routine and many habits along with it changed, the most dramatic of which was that I no longer drove from place to place. Instead, I walked. One afternoon, I stopped at a Starbucks and ordered a cappuccino. It was just the break I needed and the coffee was delicious. The original thought about stopping at a Starbucks was a conscious decision. If scientists had wired my brain then they would have seen my prefrontal cortex light up. It wasn't long before I enjoyed a cappuccino almost every afternoon. It had become a habit. Now, scientists would see another area of my brain light up.

A few months later, my husband gave me a cappuccino machine so I could enjoy my 'habit' even on days when I stayed home. Learning to use the machine was challenging at first, as I engaged my prefrontal cortex to learn all the steps. I visited the Sur La Table store several times for additional demonstrations, and after practicing day after day I learned how to use it. Now I can brew any one of four different exotic European coffee drinks while planning my talk at the library or a menu for my next dinner party.

When a habit develops, an interesting thing happens: it moves to another part of the brain, the basal ganglia, also known as the lower brain, in a specific area called the striatum. Once the habit reaches that destination it stays there forever. That doesn't mean it can't be changed, but that's no easy task. The question is: Why do habits migrate to the basal ganglia?

The main reason is that the brain is basically lazy. If it has the opportunity to funnel behaviors to a place where they become automatic, requiring little conscious thinking, it will do so in a flash. How these areas of the brain differ from each other sheds a better picture on the migration of habits.

The prefrontal cortex differs from the basal ganglia in several ways. It has been compared to the RAM memory in a computer because its capacity is finite and it burns a lot of precious fuel in the form of glucose (sugar) to do all the work that it's meant to do. But it can only hold so much information before it starts to become tired and crashes. The basal ganglia is more like the hard drive of a computer. It has greater storage capacity and is much more fuel effective. This part of the brain has many functions but for our purposes we will limit our discussion to how it stores the habits that dominate our lives. [4]

Traditionally, neuroscientists believed that once a habit is established, the conscious mind has little interaction with it. However, new studies from the Massachusetts Institute of Technology (MIT) researchers reveal that a small area of the prefrontal cortex remains alert and responsible in controlling which habits are switched on at a given time.

This is great news because it means that we have the power to put the brakes on our habits if we really put our minds to it.

Dr. Ann Graybiel, Professor at MIT, recipient of many prestigious awards, member of the McGovern Institute for Brain Research at MIT and recipient of the 2012 Kavli Prize in neuroscience, is an expert in the basal ganglia. Her work reveals that there is some piece of the cortex that is still devoted to controlling certain habitual behaviors. She says that the brain's planning centers can be responsible for shutting off some habits even if they are deeply ingrained, reinforcing the possibility that if we really **want** to make a change in our habits, we can. The operant word is **want**, which will be discussed in this chapter as we explore such concepts as willpower, motivation, and readiness for change. (5)

～

WHY ARE HABITS FORMED?

Now that we know where habits hang out, and what activates them, let's talk about why they are formed in the first place. There is a tendency to see habits in a negative way, things to get rid of or change: I have to stop smoking; I must stop eating chocolate-covered nuts; I need to stop procrastinating. The list goes on and on. But habits do serve a positive and significant purpose. They make our lives easier by removing the necessity to think of every detail of our daily existence. They give us the opportunity to execute actions effectively without having to give them much thought, thus freeing up the prefrontal cortex to express itself creatively and intellectually.

In addition, they provide us with comfort, predictability, safety and familiarity. Some habits, such as brushing our teeth, are beneficial to our health. Other habits, such as overeating, support an unhealthy life style that eventually may lead to disease of the body, mind, and spirit. Some habits are neither bad nor good. They are neutral and make up our individual idiosyncrasies and personalities. (Other habits that turn into addictions, such as alcoholism, gambling, obsessive-compulsive behaviors and many others, are considered pathological and will not be discussed in this book.)

When your habits become burdens that you carry with you and have become a part of your attitude and behaviors, remember that they are mere outcome of old decisions and you can change them through new decisions and choices.

A HABIT IS BORN

The birth of a habit starts with a cue also known as a trigger. Cues can be anything: a particular time of day, a location, other people, an emotional state, an aroma, a sound, a sight or anything at all that elicits a specific thought or behavior. The cue leads to a response, which is called a routine. The routine, in turn, provides some form of reward. The next time the same cue arises the brain remembers that reward and the behavior is repeated. When this cycle is repeated often enough and becomes automatic, the habit is born.

THE REWARD SYSTEM MADE SIMPLE

In 1954, two scientists, James Olds and Peter Milner, accidentally discovered the area in the brain responsible for the reward system while experimenting with rats. [6] They inserted electrodes in a rat's brain and stimulated the brain whenever the rat approached a certain corner, expecting the animal to stay out of that corner. Instead they observed just the opposite. The rat kept coming back to the same location, as if the brain stimulation was pleasurable. What happened was that the electrodes accidentally deviated from its intended destination and landed in the limbic system, an area of the brain primarily responsible for our emotional life, and specifically in an area of the brain that came to be known as the pleasure center. The master hormone that controls this center is dopamine. There are several dopamine pathways in the brain for various functions, but most of its pathways are part of the reward system that is directly involved in the immediate perception of the motivational component of reward.

THE ROLE OF WILLPOWER IN HABIT FORMATION

It had been a while since I had seen my friend Joan and I was looking forward to having dinner with her. I remembered how we always used to share dessert at a restaurant. I had not indulged in desserts for many years, and I had a feeling that Joan was going to try to tempt me. We met, ate a lovely dinner and then came the sticky part: "Hey Sylvie," she said, "how about sharing an éclair with me?" When I said, "I don't think so..." She gasped, "Why?" I told her that I had made some changes in my life and one of those changes was to eat healthy. She decided to order the éclair anyway, in case I changed my mind. But I didn't because I had no desire to eat the éclair. "Wow," Joan said. "What willpower you have. I wish I had it, too."

Many people believe that willpower, also referred to as self-regulation or self-control, is a character trait that either you are born with or not. Is it nature or nurture? Do we learn it from modeling our parents? How do we develop self-control? Is it something that you can count on to work all the time? These are the questions that researchers have been exploring for decades.

In the 1960's, psychologist Walter Mischel ran an experiment to test the willpower in 4 year-olds. He put a group of the children in a room where there were marshmallows in a bowl. He told them that they could have one marshmallow immediately or two marshmallows if they waited 15 minutes. He left them alone and observed their behavior. About 30% of the children who tried hard to distract themselves were able to abstain from the temptation. Later on, when they were in high school, the researchers followed up on them and found that the children who had resisted temptation were better students, scored higher on SAT tests, were more popular, and did fewer drugs. [7]

This study led to other experiments to see if willpower is a skill that can be learned. They included teaching kids tricks to distract themselves from tempting situations. The consensus was that willpower is a skill that can be acquired much the same way as learning good manners.

A hiatus in the study of willpower took place until the late 1990's when psychologist Roy Baumeister and his colleagues, Ellen Bratrslavsky, Mark Muraven, and Dianne Tice, designed an experiment that overturned the concept that willpower was just a skill to be mastered. [8]

The researchers took a team of students and put them in a room that not only smelled of chocolate cookies but also displayed them among other chocolate-flavored treats. It was chocolate heaven except for one thing: the other option was a bowlful of radishes. The team was divided into those that were to eat the chocolate cookies and those that were assigned to eat the radishes. The second part of the experiment was to see how their willpower survived. They gave all participants a standard unrelated exercise consisting of a persistence-testing puzzle, impossible to solve, until they gave up.

The results showed that the students who ate the radishes stopped doing the test puzzle much earlier than the students who ate the chocolate cookies. It seemed as if they had exhausted their self-control as they were made to eat the radishes and now their willpower was too weak to persist in trying to solve the puzzle.

That is precisely what occurred.

Additional studies led to the conclusion that willpower is like a muscle. It loses its strength, gets tired and is depleted after overuse, just like the muscles in our body fatigue after a strenuous workout. Muscles need time to recuperate and so does willpower. So, if you experience a particularly hard day at work and find yourself frustrated, suppressing angry feelings toward your boss or coworkers, and exercising your willpower to keep the peace, there's a good chance that at the end of the day you may not have enough willpower left to make healthy choices for dinner or exercise or whatever other healthy activity you might have been inclined to do otherwise. Willpower is intimately involved in all aspects of living a healthy life.

The notion that willpower had been compared to a muscle was daunting to me because I could not perceive it as a physical entity. I was just as amazed to learn that there was a relationship between glucose and self-control. Willpower not only uses glucose for its sustenance but it shares this fuel with decision-making. When glucose stores are depleted, the ability to self-regulate one's impulses are affected and decision processes are weakened.

This was very helpful information that I always keep in mind as I assist clients through special celebrations and events. I provide guidelines to follow throughout the day to minimize temptations and avoid the need to use willpower in order to preserve its strength for unpredictable events.

Bernadette, for instance, who had started her weight loss and health journey in January, was terrified about the coming holidays beginning with Thanksgiving. She was on a program of eating, every 2-3, hours, portion-controlled nutritious meal replacements and by November she had lost 70 lbs. The program was easy to implement and required very little decision making. She was scared that during the holidays she would be tempted to eat the wrong foods and that her willpower would weaken and the pounds would return. In the past, she would pretty much fast the entire day to "save" her calories for the parties she planned on attending. She would be so starved by the time she got there that she had no control over her food choices or quantities. But she didn't care because she thought she wouldn't gain weight since she had not eaten all day.

Wrong! She did gain weight.

But things were different now. She didn't have to rely on willpower anymore. Eating portion-controlled meals every 2-3 hours and drinking lots of water had become a habit. She knew from a study she had read that people who ate the same food spread out over the day lost more weight compared to those who consumed the same number of calories in one meal. [9] Armed with new information and healthy habits, Bernadette sailed through the holidays without having to access her willpower and never gained one extra.pound. You'll read more about how she did it in Chapter Six.

THE SCIENCE OF WILLPOWER

Baumeister and his team related the weakening of willpower to an energy supply that would fluctuate during the day as various events deplete and replenish it. He coined the phrase 'ego depletion' to mean the same thing as self-control depletion. Ego is a term that Sigmund Freud developed to describe the self as an energy that utilizes energy processes.

In his book *Willpower: Rediscovering the Greatest Human Strength,* co-authored with John Tierney, [10] Baumeister points out that willpower employs the same energy that is used for creative initiative, making decisions and taking action. Decision fatigue works the same way as willpower depletion. After a long day of making many decisions we tend to be less likely to want to make any more. These activities compete for the same energy supply.

However, in the October 2012 issue of *Psychology Science,* [11] researchers suggested that failure of willpower is more related to the motivational system rather than energy levels. The question is how can we figure out what is the best approach to curb our willpower. What will work for us? With these two different theories, one that empha-sizes the energy system (the relationship between glucose depletion and willpower) and another one that involves the motivational system, how do we respond? I suggest to my clients that they be prepared ahead of time with both strategies and see which one works best for them.

For example, June attends a buffet luncheon and chooses to eat a protein bar before she approaches the buffet table. The bar is low in calories but provides a certain amount of energy. Does it bolster her willpower? That's one scenario. The other choice is to seek a rewarding experience that would motivate her to activate her willpower. She could seek a friend at the event and engage in a lively conversa-tion or she could visualize herself looking thin. The best approach is for June to keep a mental list of motivational ideas that she can activate in order to put the reins on her willpower. The most important factors in both these strate-gies are awareness and mindfulness. If June can keep her goals in the forefront of her mind, either strategy will work.

If we go along with the relationship of energy being a factor in willpower sustainability then we can begin to understand why willpower diminishes when the immune system, which also uses the same energy supply, is com-promised. We can understand why willpower may deplete during premenstrual syndrome with its irritability and crav-ing for sweet or salty foods. We can understand why people with overweight issues, frustrated with countless attempts to get back to a healthy weight, succumb to a depleted self-control.

People with strong self-control experience fewer desires because they have created a habit of avoiding temptation and thus feel less guilty and stressed. They use their willpower to form good habits and break the bad ones. They have learned that avoiding temptations is better than struggling with them. In my experience, people who exercise self-control are often more successful in all aspects of life, including better relationships, less conflict and better ways to cope with stress.

Self-control gives us the opportunity to change ourselves, that is, our thoughts, focus, emotional state and impulse control, overeating and performance. Our energy supply for willpower can be replenished in a number of ways. Adopting the habits of health such as eating nutritious foods, getting 7-8 hours of restful sleep every night and taking some quiet personal time for meditating or just relaxing are some of the ways to restore self-control.

～

STRENGTHENING WILLPOWER

Like any muscle, when willpower is applied in small increments at a time when you are energetic and ready to take on a little challenge it can become stronger. Practicing willpower with small steps will help your self-control until it becomes a habit. Once it does so, it no longer requires effort to use it.

Psychologist Matthew Gailliot conducted studies showing that willpower can also improve by using the opposite, or non-dominant, hand for everyday activities such as brushing hair, opening a door or eating. [12] This technique overrides habitual ways of doing things and is useful to promote deliberate control and autonomy over our actions. (This was the catalyst for my popcorn habit mentioned earlier.)

Here's an example. Many years ago I used a program called Smokenders. I had tried everything in an attempt to stop smoking and nothing worked until I used this method.

Smokenders was a nine-week course where participants were allowed to smoke until the end of the program. We met once a week and at every meeting we changed the trigger for smoking. For instance, if a person always smoked a cigarette with his coffee, then he couldn't drink coffee and smoke at the same time. However, he could drink tea and smoke. If the habit was to hold the cigarette in the right hand between the index and the third finger, then the cigarette was held in the left hand using different fingers. If a person smoked at a bar while drinking alcohol, she was forced to choose between drinking a non-alcoholic beverage and smoking or enjoying an alcoholic drink without smoking.

At first it seemed to me that they were changing the triggers, but that wasn't the only rationale. The purpose was to override habitual ways of doing things. At the end of the nine weeks a miracle had occurred: I emerged a non-smoker. I must admit that I was able to continue on that path because I had just met the man of my life in a hospital elevator. David had suffered a heart attack and was being admitted to the coronary care unit. I was the Nursing Supervisor of Cardiac Surgery and on my way to do a pre-operative visit. David was a three pack-a-day smoker with a family and personal history of heart attack. After he was released from the hospital and we started to date, I felt a strong commitment to keep up with my decision not to smoke so as not to tempt him. This led to other discoveries. For instance, Mark Muraven's research showed that willpower was more easily recruited when people are highly motivated, be it by payment or for the good of mankind. [13] I was very motivated to keep my man away from cigarettes.

Researchers Megan Oaten and Ken Ching from Australia conducted a series of experiments in 2006 to determine whether using willpower in one area could benefit other areas. [14] The conclusion was that when willpower was strengthened in one part of life, such as exercise, the benefits spilled out to other areas of the participants' lives so that additional healthy habits were created, such as making healthy food choices.

Today, with so many choices and options available, the study of self-control is of major interest in the scientific arena. We now understand why willpower alone cannot be counted on to change habits unless we understand how it works and how to preserve it. There is no doubt that willpower affects most of our personal, social, and professional desires and is an important habit to learn because it makes a significant contribution to all areas of our lives.

MOTIVATION GETS US STARTED, HABIT KEEPS US GOING

Brandon Buchard is an American author who writes about motivation, high performance, and online marketing. In his book *The Motivation Manifesto* [15] he makes a profound statement: "The mother of motivation is choice." He refers to a motivating power within each of us that is connected with our decision to choose, a reason for action. We are either committed to that choice or we are not.

It is not enough to develop willpower to pursue your goals. It is not enough to learn methods and techniques to conquer your quest for changing habits. You must want to make a change and even that is not enough. Motivation and readiness are the driving forces needed for change to take place. To achieve a goal you need perseverance and determination to keep going, in spite of the obstacles and difficulties along the journey.

Motivation impacts every aspect of the efforts to change habits. It is the spark that sets the fire. If you are not motivated to make a change, chances are that you will not get started. And if you do get started, perhaps to satisfy someone else, the changes will probably not be successful and lasting. Motivation is what allows you to overcome obstacles to reach your goals.

No one can really motivate another person to do something. But motivation can be triggered by an inspiring moment or by a crisis in your life that beckons it.

Motivation is defined as the process that initiates, guides, and maintains goal-oriented behaviors. Some use the word "inspiration" and "motivation" synonymously. I believe that there is a slight difference between the two. Inspiration comes from the outside. Someone, something, an event or a sound can all be inspirational, but motivation stems from within. It is a feeling, an emotion that propels you to take action.

Many years ago I found myself at the crossroad of a difficult decision. I picked up a book called *The Road Less Travelled* by M. Scott Peck. [16] It inspired me and I was motivated to take action. Awareness that something needs to change is the first step to being open for inspiration. Once inspired, motivation flows and when it does it channels away the many reasons for avoiding it in the first place.

Motivation can be broken down into four areas: intrinsic and extrinsic, positive and negative. Possible combinations are internal-positive, internal-negative, external-positive and external negative. Each quadrant will provide a different kind of motivation.

Let's say that you want to quit smoking. If you are internally/positively motivated then you may be getting rid of your smoking habit because you want to be healthy. If you are internally/negatively motivated maybe you're doing it out of fear of developing emphysema or lung cancer. If you are externally/positively motivated then your reasons may be that you're the last of your friends and relatives who are quitting smoking and you want to receive the same accolades they received when they quit. If you are externally/negatively motivated maybe you're afraid of the disapproval of your family.

The three major components of motivation are activation, persistence, and intensity. In my case, enrolling in the Smokenders program was the activation stage. The fact that I stayed in the program for nine weeks showed persistence. But motivation is at the root of all change. It is such an important key to understanding human behavior that I want to provide more insight to the evolution of the various motivational theories that have been established. As you read through these various theories of motivation pay attention to which one resonates more closely to your personality.

THE INSTINCT THEORY OF MOTIVATION

The fundamental tenet of The Instinct Motivation theory, which arose in the 1950s and was developed by Konrad Lorenz and Nikolas Tinbergen, is that all living creatures are born with innate tendencies for survival. These behavioral patterns are biologically oriented and are not the result of experience or learning. It's the same motivation that drives birds to migrate or build a nest.

When I was a nursing student I rotated through the New York Foundling Home, a center for infants who had been abandoned or born from mothers who were addicts. (This center no longer exists.) After changing the diaper of one my little angels, I picked him up to give him a bottle. Suddenly, I felt something strange on my face. My little guy was sucking my cheek, seeking out a nipple to obtain nourishment. This is called the rooting reflex, another form of the Instinct Theory.

THE INCENTIVE THEORY OF MOTIVATION

The Incentive Motivation, which emerged in the 1940s, is also known as the Reward Theory. It is an outgrowth of the work done by B.F. Skinner, a famous behavioral psychologist best known for developing the theory of operant conditioning. Skinner's theory is based on the notion that a reward strengthens a behavior while punishment weakens it. As opposed to the Instinct Theory of Motivation, which has its root in innate biology, the Incentive Theory is based on the desire for positive reinforcement and rewards that are environmentally obtained. Examples are monetary, in the form of a paycheck for one's work, praise and recognition for one's accomplishments, or fulfillment of a goal.

THE DRIVE THEORY OF MOTIVATION

The Drive Theory of Motivation, also known as drive reduction theory, was developed by Clark Hull in 1943. It is based on the idea that human beings are driven by basic biological needs for food, water, shelter, and sleep to maintain homeostasis (balance) in our bodies. When a physiological need, such as hunger, arises it drives our behavior to meet those needs and so we eat to reduce the tension.

Sandra Graham and Bernard Weiner are psychologists from the University of California, Los Angeles, who have studied motivational theories in great detail. This is what they say about the Drive-reduction theory: "Drive-reduction theory also emphasizes the role that habits play in the type of behavioral response in which we engage. A habit is a pattern of behavior in which we regularly engage; once we have engaged in a behavior that successfully reduces a drive, we are more likely to engage in that behavior whenever faced with that drive in the future." [17]

THE AROUSAL THEORY OF MOTIVATION

The Arousal Theory of Motivation suggests that people are motivated to take certain actions that help them maintain an optimal level of physiological arousal. This optimal level varies from person to person, and each person has a unique level of arousal that is individual. If you have a low level of arousal you might be motivated to relax on a chaise lounge and read a book of poems. On the other hand, if your level of arousal is high, you may prefer to take a motorcycle out for a run on the highway. Personally, I am deadly afraid of heights and speed yet I love the rush that I get when I am involved in a new project that stimulates my mind and my body. Clearly, there are various degrees of arousal levels for all individuals.

The Yerkes-Dodson Law, [18] first described in 1908 by psychologists Robert Yerkes and John Dillingham Dodson, suggests that there is a relationship between performance and arousal. Increased arousal can help improve performance, but only up to a certain point. At the point when arousal becomes excessive, performance diminishes. In other words, if you are just a bit anxious about performing on an exam, on stage, or giving a speech, you will probably do better. But, if you are extremely nervous, it will hinder your results.

The Arousal Theory regards dopamine as a motivator in the body. Dopamine is the pleasure hormone contributing to the reward system that sustains our habits. Some, such as smoking, release more dopamine into the body than other habits, such a washing one's face. This is the reason that some habits are more difficult to break than others. How much dopamine is released depends on the activity of that part of the brain where dopamine is secreted, and that varies from person to person. If you like to ski, and are drawn to the more challenging slopes, chances are that the Arousal Theory motivates you. Someone with a high level of arousal may look at making changes in their lives as an exciting project whereas people with a low level of arousal may see it as a taxing and arduous project.

THE EXPECTANCY THEORY OF MOTIVATION

The Expectancy Theory of Motivation rests in the belief that we possess the capability to produce the outcome.

Victor Vroom at the Yale School of Management developed it in 1964. [19] If we feel that we lack the skills or knowledge to achieve the desired outcome we will be less motivated than someone who feels capable and confident that they can achieve their goal. Basically, the theory of expectancy is about believing in yourself and what you can achieve.

THE HUMANISTIC THEORY OF MOTIVATION

Abraham Maslow was an American psychologist whose article about the theory, entitled "A Theory of Human Motivation", was published in 1943 in *Psychological Review* [20] The hierarchy of needs exemplifies the Humanistic Theory of Motivation. It begins with the need to fulfill certain biological and physiological needs such as food and shelter; then safety, love, and esteem follow. Finally, the highest level is self-actualization, the need to fulfill one's individual potential.

WHICH OF THESE THEORIES BEST EXEMPLIFIES YOUR OWN MOTIVATION?

For me, Abraham Maslow's theory of hierarchy best describes the force that has motivated me for most of my adult life. I first encountered it in my adolescence and I remember vividly how I vowed to actualize my fullest potentials. That remains to be seen, as whenever I think I have reached my fullest potential I find ways to move forward and reach higher levels.

TAKING "MOTIVATION" TO A PREDICTABLE LEVEL

Motivation is a process with distinct levels. The Transtheoretical model, which assesses these levels, describes six distinct stages of readiness for change, ranging from no motivation or readiness to complete integration of desired change. Three clinical psychologists, Drs. James O. Prochaska, Carlo C. Diclemente and John C. Norcross, created this model in the 1980's. Their goal was to create a model that would provide guidelines for explaining behavior as a process of passing through distinct motivational stages of change. The end result of their collective fifty years of clinical research culminated in a book entitled *Changing For Good*. [21] At first the study was geared to people with addictive behaviors but in time it was easily adapted to any behavior that contradicts a person's well being. A brief description of this monumental work follows.

The first stage is called Precontemplation. In this stage, you have no intention of changing your behavior within the next six months and chances are that you're denying that you have a problem in the first place, although you can also be aware of a problem but not ready to deal with it.

Monica was a procrastinator and drove John, her boy-friend, crazy. This led to many arguments between them. "You have this habit of leaving everything for the last minute," he would shout at her. "That's not a habit," she would answer back. "And there is nothing wrong with that," she insisted. "You're the one that is compulsive about getting things done right away." And so they bickered, back and forth. Clearly, the first step to move on to the other stages is awareness. Monica didn't see her procrastination as a problem or a bad habit and she didn't think it might ever jeopardize her job, but it did. Losing a job that she loved jolted her enough to put her on to the next stage of readiness.

The next stage is called Contemplation. Now you are aware that a problem exists and you're getting ready to make a change. You're thinking about doing something about it but you're not quite sure how. Monica recognized that her procrastination was indeed a bad habit and that maybe she should do something about it.

The next category is the Preparation stage. Here you are ready to make a change and you intend to do so within the next 30 days. You may even start making some small changes as you gain knowledge and you're setting up a plan of action. As for Monica, she started a journal and listed one task to do every day of the week. For example, the first day she would straighten out her shoes in the closet. The second day she would contact a friend she had not seen in a while. Little by little she got used to planning something and attending to it right away. She asked John to be her accountability partner and he was thrilled to comply.

The following stage is called Action. You are finally actively engaged in changing your behavior but for a period of less than six months. Monica was focused on following her schedule in attending to her chores. She continued to journal her activities and rely on John for feedback.

The fifth stage is referred to as Maintenance. You have been engaged in the new behavior for at least six months. Now Monica was no longer procrastinating. She was enjoying a better relationship with John and started looking for another job.

The last stage is called Termination. You reached your goal! You achieved complete change in your behavior and you can't even imagine yourself with the old unwanted habits that ran your life. Monica found a new job. And what's more important is that since she no longer procrastinated, Monica's life was much more organized and she found more time in her hands to do many other activities she could never get to before.

The Transtheoretical model provides a series of self-assessment questionnaires that are extremely helpful in determining what stage you are on. People who are self-changers and motivated to understand their behaviors will be particularly drawn to taking this self-assessment.

Are you contemplating a change in your life? If so, where do you see yourself belonging in the Transtheoretical model?

It's important to remember that these stages of readiness seldom follow a linear fashion; you can go back and forth for a while before you reach your goal. It's not unusual for most people to need several recycles before they completely change their behavior.

CHAPTER THREE:

Many Habits, Many Methods

Everyone, in every walk of life, grapples with habits they want to conquer. No matter what their level of education, financial status, or age—no one is exempt. Perhaps it takes close friendships for people to admit they want to make a change and can't do it so easily. By bringing the habit out in the open and sharing our own personal stories and experiences, we become more aware of our own needs to making lifestyle changes.

That's why I always look forward to attending a bi-yearly reunion, a custom that started several years ago. We are an eclectic group: a college professor, a lawyer, an editor, an artist, a financial advisor, an interior decorator, a CEO of a business company, and me. The highlight of our meeting is our "lunch and learn" time. We reserve a back room at a restaurant, which gives us plenty of time to eat, catch up and delve into our discussion. The last time our topic was ways to create or change habits.

KINDEL'S STORY

Kindel started the discussion. A vibrant brunette all of 5'2 and an eldercare lawyer, is married and has two lovely teenage daughters who were falling into a pattern of drinking diet soda. Kindel was very much aware that drinking water was a healthier habit than drinking soda. Unfortunately, she was not a good example. She had to make that her habit so she could be a better role model for her girls.

"Drinking water has always been difficult for me," she began. "There was no problem getting my fluids from other sources but when it came to just plain water I couldn't bring myself to do it. I was raised in an old-fashioned European family who believed that water was for bathing and not for drinking. But I knew better. I had the idea of filling a pitcher with 64oz of water and pouring some of it in bottles that I could carry around at all times. But I kept forgetting to drink. By the end of day one my pitcher was three-quarters full and the rest of the week was no better. I could see that I would need help so I decided to discuss my challenges with a friend who is also a health coach. She told me that there are several methods to help people change their habits and she recommended a few books. In the course of my research, I came across the Fogg Method.

(22) It totally resonated with me because it was simple and to the point. The Fogg Method is based on the principle of one baby step at a time. Dr. B.J. Fogg, a Stanford University professor, behaviorist and founder of the Persuasive Tech Lab, created it. He named his technique Tiny Habits.

"Fogg's system for starting a new habit or changing an old one is based on three simple steps. The first one is to be **specific**. The second step is to make it **easy** and the third is to set a **trigger.** The well-known example that he lectures about frequently is on the habit of dental flossing. If someone wants to make dental flossing a habit he tells the person to only floss one tooth because that is a **specific** goal. The **trigger** would be to place the dental floss right next to the toothbrush since brushing teeth was already an established habit. The idea is that once the flossing habit is formed it is easy to keep on flossing another tooth and then another until it becomes a habit to floss all teeth in conjunction with brushing them.

"Here's how I followed this system. The first thing I did was to be more specific with my goal. I set myself up to drink one sip of water every half hour. I made it easy by setting a reminder and an alert on my phone plus carrying a water bottle at all times. I added an additional trigger by putting a bottle of water as a background picture on my cell phone and computer. Every time I took one sip of water I gave myself a pat in the back and told myself what a great job I was doing. Within two months, I was chugging close to a liter of water a day. My girls were so impressed that they decided to follow my act. My husband, on the other hand, is still thinking about it. We're working on him."

MAUREEN'S STORY

The attractive 43 year-old redhead, a skillful financial advisor, spoke next.

"I desperately needed to change my clutter habit. I am the youngest of six children, all the rest boys, and was raised in a large house in Connecticut. My parents were architects and worked out of the house. I couldn't tell whether they were neatness challenged or just lacked the time and energy to create a well-ordered environment. It was just a happy home that lacked discipline. I attended a college nearby and graduated first in my class as a financial advisor. I got married soon after but the marriage ended in divorce. I was never quite sure why but later I entertained the possibility that perhaps the clutter in my home played a part in that outcome. My ex-husband was a quiet man who rarely expressed his thoughts and feelings until one day, just before Christmas, he told me he no longer wanted to be married to me.

"At first I was devastated and completely clueless. Gradually I came out of my shell and started to date again.

Soon I began to notice a trend. Things would go well with my dates until I brought them to my apartment. After that they would disappear. Finally, I got the message: My cluttered home was turning these men off. I decided that if I was going to have a meaningful relationship, I needed to do something about this bad habit. I remembered from a course I once took in Feng Shui that clutter was a major disruption in the energy of an environment and could affect the destiny of a relationship. I thought about hiring a professional organizer but common sense dictated that what I really needed was to learn how to be neat. So I embarked on a mission to discover how I could change my clutter habit. It was the beginning of a new year and I decided to make a resolution to be neat and organized. I attended a talk given by Caroline Arnold, author of *small move, big change.* [23] She created a system called Microresolutions, which is similar to the Tiny Habits that Kindel just described in that both focus on specific, targeted behaviors, taking baby steps and making them easy to do.

"I was overwhelmed with all the changes I thought I would be forced to make in order to reach my goal to be neat. But what I learned from attending Arnold's lecture, and later on from reading her book, was that I had to switch my mindset from being neat to doing the one thing that would get me closer to my goals. The emphasis was on breaking down the tasks to bitable sizes and repeating them until they were done mindlessly. Unless you're repeating the same routine over and over again, it won't become second nature, it won't come automatically, and it won't become a habit. Another important factor for success was learning to reinforce my new habit by sending myself a mental message along with that behavior change.

"I started my first microresolution by hanging up my clothing when I came home from work. My self-message was 'my clothes won't be as wrinkled if I hang them up right away.' I followed this routine for a few weeks until it was on autopilot. Once I began to hang up my clothing mindlessly without having to think about it, I moved on to my next 'neat' goal. It took about four weeks to feel ready for my next action step, which was to load the dishwasher on Fridays so my kitchen would be more organized for the weekend. I could always load the dishwasher more often if I wanted to but the rule to measure and celebrate my success was based on accomplishing the task on Fridays.

"Soon I began to find pleasure in my micro accomplishments. Because each one initiated greater momentum for the next change, I started to move on, with greater ease and speed, to other areas of my home that needed help. Gradually, by examining the areas I wanted to improve and taking some baby steps, my habits began to change. It took me nine months to form these new habits and now I can't understand how I could have lived in that chaos. Best of all, I am no longer embarrassed to invite my friends to my apartment, and my dates aren't disappearing."

REGINA'S STORY

Regina, at 39, an accomplished freelance commercial artist who specializes in murals for the home and office, followed:

"My bingeing started soon after Johnnie was born. Three years later, after Susie's birth, I noticed a few additional undesirable pounds creeping up. I got scared. I saw myself with a bad habit that could lead to more serious weight gain and decided to take action. I started journaling to identify my bingeing habit more closely. This is what I discovered: I had no problem during the day when I was busy with art projects, housework, and taking care of the kids. It was in the evening, after dinner, when all hell broke loose. Just when I would find a few minutes to relax and watch TV I started snacking and, in no time, I realized that I had eaten a whole bag of potato chips or a pint of ice cream or a handful of chocolate chip cookies. Why have all these foods in the house? Well, with kids and a husband who can eat and eat without gaining weight, I couldn't avoid it. A friend told me that what helped her stop her bingeing was taking a walk alone or with her family after dinner. When I suggested it to my family they looked at me like I was crazy. So I took walks by myself and when I got home I found myself reaching for more snacks. Well, that wasn't going to work. I remembered that knitting was always a focusing and meditative hobby for me so I tried to do that but it still didn't curb my cravings for snacks. It was time to seek professional help.

"I tried hypnosis and various other kinds of psycho-therapies, ranging from analytical to behavioral. Nothing helped. Then I read Charles Duhigg's book *The Power of Habits* [24]*)* and decided to follow his Framework for changing habits, using the habit loop that MIT research-ers had developed to explain how habits are formed. If you're not familiar with the Habit Loop, let me explain: The loop consists of three parts: a cue, a routine and a reward. A cue can be anything: food, drinks, an aroma, a sight, a sound, and a time of day. The cue triggers a behavior, referred to as a routine, and a reward follows. Next time the clue shows up you consciously repeat the routine, which continues to reward you. When the routine becomes automatic it has graduated to a 'habit.' Using this concept of the habit loop, Mr. Duhigg created a Framework that includes four steps: 1. Identifying the routine, 2. Experimenting with the rewards, 3. Isolating the cue, and 4. Having a plan. This made sense to me and I decided to try it. My cue occurred right after din-ner. My routine was to binge. My reward was, as my son Johnnie would describe it: Yummy. I experimented with different scenarios and questioned myself: Was I still hun-gry after dinner? Was I tired or did I need to exercise? Did I need a break from all the responsibilities of the day? I experimented with all these possibilities but saw no change in my bingeing. I almost gave up this method when, one day, Johnnie came home with a jigsaw puzzle he had gotten at a birthday party. We decided to play with it after dinner, and guess what happened! That's right, after a while of playing it I realized it: I was no longer bingeing!

"For me, focusing on an activity that involved my whole family, where everyone was having fun, was the key to getting my mind off snacking."

RENEE'S STORY

Renee, at 67 elegant as always in a suit and heels, and a retired CEO of a dress manufacturing company, took her turn.

"I could never resist jewelry. I was just as attracted to expensive jewelry as the more commercial and cheaper ones, which gave my husband Rick some relief since I bought an average of 4 to 6 pieces a week. Sometimes I returned or exchanged them, but mostly I kept them. I was blessed with friends who took turns accompanying me to these shopping sprees, but truth be told, I didn't need anyone to come with me. If the stores had been opened 24 hours a day I would have been there in a flash on a sleepless night. It was obvious that it had become a habit. For many years, I was not motivated to change my shopping behavior. I could afford it, my husband tolerated it, and I had many friends who took turns shopping with me so that it didn't affect any of our relationships. I continued to accumulate earrings, watches, necklaces and especially bracelets until one day a major alteration in my life became the catalyst for changing my behavior.

"Rick died. I was devastated. I left my job and moved to Texas to be closer to my daughter and my two grandchildren. Throughout my grieving process buying jewelry was the furthest thing from my mind. I had read somewhere that a change in environment is often the cause for habits to change and new ones to form. In my case, I turned to making a new home for myself and getting to know my grandchildren better. I feel very liberated from the frenzy of my habit. I never realized how much energy it took to constantly shop and how little I had left for other things. I am so much more at peace with myself now. For me, changing my habit was a spiritual experience."

MIRIAM'S STORY

Miriam was next to share her story. At 53 a professor of quantum physics at a university in her hometown, she is the group's appointed intellectual.

"As you all know, I had a bad habit of interrupting. Many of you pointed this out to me several times, and I remember always finding excuses for why I did it. I probably would still be interrupting today if it weren't for the fact that I experienced a very embarrassing and uncomfortable meeting with my boss. One day, the Dean of my department called me to set up a meeting. I couldn't imagine what he wanted to discuss with me. I arrived a little early and a bit nervous. He used the utmost tact when he told me that many of my students and co-workers complained about my constant interruptions. I was stunned. Even though I had been told many times that I was a chronic interrupter, I tended to ignore it. Well, this time I took it more seriously. I faced it head on, admitted it, and decided to do something about it. I knew there were several techniques for changing habits so I embarked on a mission to find the right match for me. A colleague recommended Art Markman's book *Smart Change.* [25]

"For me it was the answer to changing my habit. Reading the book gave me a glimpse into how my habit might have started. I grew up in a home with intellectual and extroverted parents and four siblings. None of them ever stopped talking. As the youngest, the only way I could get a word in edgewise in the conversation was to interrupt. Actually, everybody interrupted each other. Throughout my adult life I often sensed that people avoided socializing with me. In the past I didn't place too much importance to an occasional constructive criticism about it. Now things were different; I began to examine my relationships and started to understand the impact this habit might be having on others.

"Markman explores the motivational system that helps us achieve our goals and identifies two systems for reaching them. One is called the Go System. This is our personal habit-creation machine. It takes the behavior that we originally think about and transitions it to an automatic habit. It's the system that drives our behavior. The other is the Stop System, which prevents us from giving in to our temptations. This is the system that needs to recognize the behavior we don't want and stops it from happening. Markman identifies certain tools to help change behavior.

"The first action step is to 'optimize the goal' which means to describe our new goal in specific terms citing the when, where, and how that action will take place. Using the Smart Change Journal I wrote the following: 'Every Monday morning (from 8 am to 10 am) while at work, if someone is talking to me, I will listen attentively and count silently until 10 before I talk to them. Once that starts to feel natural I will increase one day every week and repeat the same behavior.'

"Next, I needed to learn to tame the 'Go' System by identifying my triggers for interrupting and replacing them with new ones and generating specific plans to deal with obstacles. My trigger was fairly easy to identify as I only interrupted when other people were talking.

"Now I was ready to move on to harness the 'Stop' System. This system goes in place when stress arises that might lead into the temptation to revert back to the old habit. I knew that if I could learn to handle my stress I was less likely to fall back to my old habits. I decided to practice the deep breathing I had learned in yoga class. At first I did it three times a week in the afternoon at 3 pm when I knew I would have a break in the day. Gradually it became a habit that I use whenever I face stress.

"I found the book to be an excellent guide through the process of changing my habit. I had a few other habits I wanted to change and promised myself to tackle them once my interrupting habit was completely eliminated."

LAUREN'S STORY

Lauren, who offered to speak next, is, at 50, a busy artist and interior decorator. The habit she focused on was her sensitivity to people's criticism, especially when it was work related.

"I always felt hurt and angry whenever someone disagreed with my designs. I would send all kinds of negative thoughts to myself that affected my creativity and productivity. One day I was working on decorating a living room for a client that I had been occupied with for a while. The client was not happy with the location of the sofa and when she mentioned it I snapped at her. This was the first time I had ever let my feelings known and it almost cost me the loss of my client.

"I was alarmed. I needed to know why I reacted that way. Did it always have to be my way? Rationally, I understood that people are entitled to their opinions. Why was I so sensitive to these issues? I was going to get to the bottom of this before it got out of hand. I went to a few sessions with a psychotherapist where I had a chance to talk about my childhood. I was the only child of parents who were art professors. They were very strict when it came to my schoolwork and later on, at college, my artwork. One time my father tore up a watercolor that I had spent a lot of time painting because it wasn't perfect. It crushed me. I was depressed and angry for a long time after that. I thought that my present behavior stemmed from my upbringing and that knowing this I could correct it. But that didn't happen. One day, I came across an article that mentioned 'emotional habit,' a completely different perspective that I had never considered. From then on I read everything I could get my hands on about habits.

"Of all the research I did the one method that resonated best with me was a book written by Dave Sellars, PhD called *Stop or Start Habits*. [26] I liked it because it was straightforward with practical, easy-to-follow, step-by-step applications. According to Dr. Sellars, to make it an action, a stop-the-habit goal must begin with the word *Stop* or *Start*. I was motivated to write my goals in a journal with a statement that I found in the appendix of the book: 'Start accepting that it is OK for me not to be perfect.' I experimented with a few other goal affirmations, some of which were written in the book and others that were my own, such as 'start being aware of my emotions and recognize constructive criticism without necessarily having to agree with it.'

"I liked the concept of recognizing the difference between 'rational thought' and 'emotions,' and understanding that logic and reason begs for change but motivation comes from emotion. For me, a rational benefit for changing would be satisfied clients, increased referrals, and a boost in my business. Emotionally, I would benefit by feeling confident in my work regardless of any changes my client requests.

"What I loved most about this book was the Outcome-Visioning, a technique created by Dr. Sellars. Outcome-Visioning is a combination of meditation, hypnosis, affirmations and creative visualization that focuses on the desired end itself. I was familiar with creative visualization because I used it in my work all the time. Before the pencil went to the drawing board I would conceive and visualize the entire project in my mind. Not sure whether I would succeed or not, using this method to change my habit I was relieved to see a chapter on how to handle slip-ups and relapses. This book worked very well for me. I love my new 'cool, calm, and collected' attitude even in the presence of temperamental clients."

MARGARITA'S STORY

Margarita, at 36 an associate editor of a fashion magazine, spoke up next.

"I don't remember when my Facebook habit started. All I know is that I was checking my Facebook page at least 10 times per hour. I didn't even realize it until one of my co-workers warned me that the boss was keeping an eye on me. I got worried because I loved my job and I didn't want to do anything to jeopardize it. Then I remembered that one of my friends had poor sleeping habits and found a way to change it. I asked her how she did it and my friend referred me to the work of Amy Johnson, a psychologist and a life coach. Her book, *The Little Book of Change*, [27] offers a unique perspective about habits, namely, 'Your habit is not YOU. It's your brain.' Amy explains that our habits have nothing to do with who we are. They are not a reflection of our character and have little, if anything, to do with our past. She blames it all on the brain, which is part of us much the same as our finger is part of us but is not all of who we are. The brain forms the habit and we are just the recipients of the experience that habit brings.

"An urge is nothing more than a thought and thoughts are always temporary. Here comes the crux of how we can change our habits according to this model: If we don't obey those urges and act upon them, the urge fades and the habit will eventually disappear. It takes practice, and there could be setbacks, but it doesn't matter. They are not a big deal as long as we understand that they are meaning-less and only a part of the process.

"You may think you need will power to do that but you really don't. Actually, when you're using your willpower you are adding more thought to the mix and that confuses the issue. When the urge to look at Facebook came on, I ignored it long enough for the urge to go away. It actually worked for me! To date, my habit has diminished to twice a day, which is acceptable. As I continue to work on my higher brain to make the decision not to act upon the urge to check Facebook, I'm on my way to giving up a habit that might have cost my job."

MY TURN

After I told my friends that I had embarked on a new career and was writing a book, I shared the following story.

"No matter where I was with my writing, come 5PM, I closed the computer and headed to the kitchen to start dinner, but not before pouring myself a glass of wine. I hadn't always done that. So many of my jobs didn't allow me to get home that early. But when I started to work from home my routine changed.

"My schedule was to work in the morning from 7 to 11. Then I took an exercise class from 11 to 12, ate lunch from 12:30 to 1:30 and got back to my desk by 2 to write for another 3 hours. Sometimes I'd drink the wine at 5 PM even when I wasn't in the mood for it and even if I wasn't cooking dinner. After observing my habit for a few months, my husband Dave said, 'I think you're becoming a little bit of an alcoholic.' 'Is that like being a little bit pregnant?' I replied.

"I know that I'm not an alcoholic, and I realized that wine at 5 was a habit, not an addiction. An addiction is a habit that's gone out of control and is reinforced by a craving that is not always satisfied. My habit was satisfied with one glass of wine. Sometimes I'd skip it altogether and, once in a while, I would enjoy another glass with the meal. Nonetheless, Dave's comment hit a nerve. I wondered why I started this habit and after giving it much thought realized that what I needed at that time was a break from writing.

"In the morning when I quit writing I went to an exercise class. That relaxed me and set the stage for another

3 hours of writing. It's a good habit and I realized that I needed the same break in the afternoon when I was ready to relax. Cooking helps me to unwind and a glass of wine brings out my culinary creativity. Still, I was curious to see if I could break the wine habit. So, for several weeks, I put on my running shoes and ran for about a mile before starting dinner. That worked just as well as the wine and I was tickled that I could prove to Dave that I wasn't an alcoholic. And I was just as pleased to drink a glass of wine when I felt like it."

COMMON THREADS

There is an underlying common thread in most of the information shared about my friends' habits. Most researchers and authors advocate writing "s.m.a.r.t." goals (specific, measurable, achievable, realistic, and time framed). Everyone agreed on the importance of acting on one change at a time and concentrating on small steps until they became second nature. They all referred to core habits that would give way to smaller wins. There were other similarities, such as rewarding oneself for each small accomplishment, keeping a journal to track success and stating goals in a positive tone. They all talked about triggers, motivation, will power, awareness and mindfulness.

However, each method had its own spin and appeal to the personalities of those interested in making a positive change in their habits. Finding the one that is best suited for each individual was the key to a successful outcome.

In the next chapter you'll read about strategies and approaches to change your habits, provided that you are ready and willing to embark on this new phase of your life. My Triple A 's of Body, Mind, and Spirit for starting healthy habits and changing the unhealthy ones will be introduced.

CHAPTER FOUR:

The Triple A's of Body, Mind, and Spirit

Choosing the right method to form a new habit or change an old one is all about trial and error. There is no one way that works for everyone and for all habits. A method that works for one habit may not work for another one even for the same person. Sometimes it's a combination of methods that work best; at other times, no established technique works except the one that you make up yourself.

A method that works for a habit that involves the act of "doing" something automatically, such as smoking, hanging up clothing, bingeing, or biting nails, may not work for a habit that is expressed mentally, such as multi-tasking, worrying, punctuality or laziness.

Some habits change overnight when a life-threatening experience relates to them. For instance, as I mentioned

earlier, my husband David smoked three packs of cigarettes a day until he suffered a heart attack. He survived
the crisis and never touched a cigarette again. (It doesn't
always have to be such a dramatic experience. I knew
that I should brush my dogs' teeth regularly but it took a
$600 bill from my vet for teeth cleaning for me to get into
the habit of brushing Bo and Bella's teeth every day. I was
immensely rewarded when my vet told me Bella's teeth
looked great one year later. Bo never needed professional
cleaning since I started him on the right path early on.)

Eleanor had quit her habit of biting her nails primarily by using Charles Duhigg's Framework that incorporated
the Habit Loop. Because it had worked so well she was
disappointed and surprised that it didn't work for her annoying and socially disturbing new habit. She would start
every sentence with the word "so." This was particularly
exasperating when she was giving presentations for her
advertising firm. "I sound like a teenager," she claimed.
This may not sound like a bad habit but it was annoying
and it detracted her from giving a smooth and professional
performance.

Eleanor was confident that if she could stop nail biting, which had been ingrained since childhood, surely she
could change this habit in half the time. Not so. She tried
a series of other techniques but none helped. Frustrated
with the whole thing she decided to meditate, let it go and
focus on her breathing. That didn't work either. Then she

had an idea to write out her presentation word for word and rehearse it as often as possible. Two weeks later she noticed that she wasn't saying "so" anymore. Why did she pick up this habit in the first place? She had done this presentation hundreds of times and didn't need notes, but she had gotten so accustomed to giving it that her mind, at times, would wander. Writing her talk made her more aware and mindful of what she wanted to say. Now she was focused and no longer filled her sentences with the word 'so' either in her work or in her social interactions. Since then, Eleanor has experienced inner calmness and more enjoyment in her everyday life. Was it because she had conquered her "so" habit? Maybe, but that wasn't all. It was adopting the habit of "awareness and mindfulness" that changed her life.

If you are disturbed about any other habitual language and communication habit such as "you know" or "like", try keeping a log of how often you are using them. You can easily do this with a check mark and note the occasion of usage. This will enhance your awareness.

MY OWN EXPERIENCE

I can relate to Eleanor's unwanted habit. Many years ago the words "okey dokey" dominated my vocabulary. I used them constantly, even as an operating room nurse.

Every time the surgeon asked for an instrument, instead of just clapping it into her hand I automatically said the two words. This irritated the surgical team so much they gave me an ultimatum: get rid of that expression or don't work with us anymore. I explained that it had become a habit and asked them to give me some time to find a way to get rid of it. They gave me two weeks.

The first thing I did was to ask my family and friends to immediately let me know when I was using that expression. Then I devised my own aversion technique by biting my tongue every time I said "okey dokey." The sense of urgency and the sore tongue helped, but, most importantly, I became very much aware of my speech. I got rid of the habit within two weeks.

BE AWARE AND MINDFUL

If you're not aware and mindful that you have a habit that needs to change, or a new habit that needs to develop, then no technique in the world will make that change happen. If you're not ready to make an alteration in your behavior no technique you use will last.

Intention is the plan or the idea that gets awareness and mindfulness started.

THE ROLE OF AWARENESS

Awareness implies a mental, conscious recognition that brings about insight, understanding, and knowledge. It's the "I get it" moment that puts it all together and opens the door to enlightenment and interest in a particular situation or development.

There are several levels of awareness.

One level of awareness is the social one that focuses on the external, the world of reality. It is the world as other people experience it. For instance:

✓ July is the month for Melanoma **Awareness.**

✓ The increase in violent attacks in schools has caused **awareness** about gun control.

✓ Attacks against Jews in Europe have increased **awareness** of anti-Semitism.

✓ There's increased **awareness** of people who are homeless.

The other area of awareness is both internal and personal. For instance:

✓ You lost 30 pounds and aware that people are noticing.

✓ You are aware that you're tired and edgy.

✓ You are aware that you drink, eat and/or worry too much.

✓ You have habits you don't like.

A deeper level of awareness is the internal and expanded one which brings on mindfulness. You're not only aware but you also question your reasons, motives, and rationale for what you are aware of. Mindfulness is paying attention and focusing on your thoughts, feelings, bodily sensations, and your environment as you are going through an experience at a particular moment in time.

As Deepak Chopra has stated so elegantly in his meditation series, "As you begin your awareness you gain ultimate power and freedom...you can start dissolving old habits and create new choices...the most important victory is your connection to awareness." [28]

To create new habits, or change the old ones no longer working for you, you'll need awareness, mindfulness, and readiness, the triple mindset to get ready for action and a plan of action for accomplishing your goal.

This is the level of awareness that is called for in the Triple A's of Body, Mind, and Spirit.

THE TRIPLE A'S OF BODY, MIND, AND SPIRIT

No matter what method or technique you use for creating and changing your habits you must begin with expanded **awareness**. This kind of awareness will put you in charge of your life and bring freedom from your bad habits. The specific method or methods that you choose are the tools to implement the action steps that follow the expanded awareness.

The Triple A's of body, mind, and spirit that I have created consists of three parts:

1. Awareness

2. Action

3. Accountability

Awareness: You recognize the need for changing a habit, for instance, you are looking to learn new and healthier habits. Ask yourself and write down:

1. Am I ready for change?

2. Which habit do I want to acquire or change first?

3. Why do I want to acquire or change this habit?

4. How will the new habit affect my body, mind, and spirit?

5. How will the new habit affect those around my family, my friends and me?

6. Who can I share my awareness and plan of action with?

Expanded awareness leads to investigating ways to act upon what you want to change.

Action: On the bottom of a sheet of paper write just one habit that you want to change. Next to it, write your "why:" Why do you want to change that habit? Why do you want to acquire a new one? Next to your "why" write how your habit is affecting your body, mind, and spirit. Then, at the top of the sheet, write the new habit you want to acquire and how it will change your life. In the middle, write down the specific method/technique you plan to use to acquire or change your new habit.

Accountability: Changing habits or creating new ones requires commitment. Being held accountable in order to reach your goals is paramount for success.

Some habits are more difficult to change than others. If you're just moving the location of an item it may take a week or two before you automatically head for that location without thinking about it. Other habits may take longer, especially those that have been ingrained for a long time and for those that bring a great deal of pleasure, such as eating chocolate.

Most people struggle to get rid of their habits.

Let's say that you want to get rid of your candy habit because you're putting on weight. You may start off very motivated and enthusiastic about your decision, which is great because that's going to propel you to get full steam to accomplish your goal. You have emptied your house of all trace of candy, and you have asked your friends to not even say the word chocolate in front of you. You decide on an action plan, a particular method that you think will work for you, and you implement it. You're doing well for a couple of weeks until a stressful event occurs. Without accountability to someone for your decision, you find yourself succumbing to the sweets that had given you such comfort in the past.

When you are accountable to someone it requires you to accept responsibility for your actions and stay true to your goals. Accountability is particularly important when you get started and when you hit roadblocks that try to derail you from your goals. That's when you wish you had someone you could call to stop you from regressing to old habits. You need someone who would challenge, motivate, mentor, encourage and inspire you to achieve maximum results.

WHO SHOULD BE YOUR ACCOUNTABILITY PARTNER?

When looking for the right accountability partner there are options:

- ✓ Professional coaches. These can be paid life coaches, health coaches, and fitness trainers. Many health programs that assist people to reach a healthy weight and change their lifestyles provide free health coaches in their plan. The advantage of being accountable to a professional coach is that they can also act as consultants in other areas of your goals and guide you to the different methods for changing habits.

- ✓ A friend, a co-worker, a family member, or even someone you have never met but have established a relationship of trust and respect via social media. Pick someone you can be honest and open with and who will, in turn, give you honest and open feedback without judgment. It can be a young adult or even an older child who has earned your respect as a conscientious person. What I like about working with a young adult is that it can be a win-win situation for both parties. Knowing that you are expected to report your progress each week can be motivating for you and a great learning experience for the youngster.

Key qualities to look for in an accountability partner:

✓ Seek someone who is reliable, who can be reached quickly and who will respond rapidly. This person should be someone that you can talk to on a regular basis, preferably weekly or more often if necessary.

✓ Make sure that they are willing and excited about being your accountability partner. As much as possible, pick someone who can relate to your goals at some level. It is not necessary for them to experience the same habits as yours but they must be able to understand your struggle.

✓ Choose someone that you can be comfortable talking to and be open about your struggles and who will give you honest and open feedback. Reassure them that you need them to hold you to your commitment when you waiver.

Your accountability partner does not need to be a permanent fixture in your life. Once you feel secure that you have reached your goals to change a habit or create a new one, you can let them go.

My personal approach to forming most habits or changing bad ones is a technique I call the **Mantra Habit.** It is about giving yourself a subliminal suggestion before going to sleep, or any other time, during the course of changing or creating a habit. This is done over a period of at least 30 days.

THE MANTRA HABIT

I created the Mantra Habit as a concept for change to begin from a deeper energy center using subliminal suggestions. The background for the creation took place many years ago when I was taking Tai Chi classes as part of my curriculum in acupuncture school. We didn't start the Tai Chi form until our minds and bodies were ready.

First, we sat in a comfortable position on the floor with our legs crossed. The purpose was to quiet our minds so that we could access the main center of energy, which in Chinese philosophy is in the lower part of the belly, called the Tan Tien. Next, we performed a series of exercises such as Push Hands Practice to acquire control of our energy. Then we took a standing position and worked on our body alignment until the teacher had checked each of the 30 students in the class and then gave the command: "Commence Tai Chi."

What came out of this practice, that eventually led me to create my Mantra Habit, is the concept that before we can put our energies forward in a physical way we must mentally be prepared for it. The Li (intention) precedes the Qi (the energy to act upon that intention).

I started using the Mantra Habit when I was a practicing Chiropractor. Many of my patients suffered with neck pain and stiffness. It turned out that most of them slept on their stomach. The sustained strain on the neck from that position would aggravate their condition because the cervical spine needs proper support to maintain its natural curve. However, it seemed almost impossible for them to change their habits. I suggested that they give themselves a subliminal message every night, for 21 days, before going to sleep.

THE 21-DAY THEORY

Somewhere along the way I heard about the 21-day theory to form a new habit or break a bad one. The 21-day myth started in the 1950's when a plastic surgeon, Dr. Maxwell Maltz, noticed that patients who had rhinoplasty surgery—a nose job—took 21 days to get used to seeing their new face. Patients with amputations also took about 21 days of sensing a phantom limb before adjusting to the new situation. He began to look into his own behavior and concluded, "It requires a **minimum** of about 21 days for an old mental energy to dissolve and a new one to jell." He wrote about this observation in his book *Psycho-Cybernetics*. [29] Eventually people began to omit the word "minimum" and accepted it as fact.

Then, in 2009, psychologist researcher Phillippa Lally conducted a study [30] that revealed that it takes anywhere between 18 to 254 days for people to form a new habit, and an average of 66 days before a new behavior becomes automatic.

Based on this information I devised a mantra that my patients would repeat for a minimum of 30 days, preferably before going to sleep although it could be used at other situations. The mantra was to be phrased in a positive way and would affirm what they were going to do to avoid sleeping on their stomach. For example, it would say: I will always sleep on my back or on my side every night. The trick was that they were to repeat the sentence, accentuating each word of the sentence every time: **I** will always sleep on my back or my side every night. I **will** always sleep on my back or my side every night. I will **always** sleep on my back or my side every night. I will always **sleep** on my side or my back every night. And so forth. By emphasizing a different word in the sentence, the mantra cannot be repeated automatically so that it forces you to focus on your goal. What I found was that most of my patients who used this method reported that they rarely found themselves sleeping on their stomachs when they practiced this technique. I was overjoyed to have found a way to change this unhealthy habit.

We tend to forget that as difficult as it is to break our bad habits they were still created by us. Therefore we have the power to break them and create new ones. Remember that habits are created so we can do things automatically, without awareness. To get rid of our bad habits is to bring awareness back into our minds. To do that we need to conquer the "monkey noise" (the constant chatter) that often dominates our minds.

Mastering the art of meditation will bring the stillness needed to dig deeply within and find your way into awareness. Exercises such as Yoga and Tai Chi harness your focus on your breath and energies, releasing tension in your body and freeing yourself of the mindless chatter in your brain. And you can always "talk" to your monkey brain and let it know who's the boss.

"By recognizing thoughts that are not true but are habits, we begin to affirm our positive truths and move towards a more satisfied, whole place. Self awareness has the power to affirm our truths and free us from unconscious behaviors." –Oprah Winfrey [31]

THE WHOLISTIC NATURE OF HABITS

As an Acupuncturist I see the body and mind as one inter-connected entity. Each affects the other. Many habits begin as a thought that, in turn, affects the body and the spirit.

A habit, such as overeating, may appear to only affect the body and potentially contribute to obesity, heart disease, high blood pressure, and some forms of cancer. But how the mind responds may be just as detrimental with feelings of guilt, inadequacy, embarrassment, and poor self-image.

WORRYING

A certain amount of worrying is normal. You fret about your kids when they aren't home by a certain hour. You're concerned when someone you love is not looking well and may be sick. You sweat about how you're going to pay the rent when cash flow is poor. Worrying is a sign of a sense of responsibility and some degree of maturity. Excessive worry, however, falls in the category of an obsessive habitual behavior that serves no purpose and causes anxiety. Like many other personality traits, it's the degree of the behavior that moves it from normal to abnormal. If you are someone who worries too much about all things, rest assured that you can get rid of this bad habit. For our purposes, the term "worry" or "worrier" is designated to mean "excessive worry."

Pauline is a worrier. She started her worrying habit when she was in college. An overachiever and an excellent student, she constantly agonized about her grades. She had good study habits and was always prepared for exams, yet she would walk away from every test with gloom and doom and worried herself sick until she got her grades back. And, of course, they were all A's.

She graduated from college with a Bachelor's degree in biology and continued her studies to become a surgical Physicians' Assistant. After she accepted a position in a prestigious teaching hospital her worrying habit accelerated considerably: "What if I work too slowly, cut an important vessel, or ignore a patient's allergies?" "What if?" was a persistent question that haunted her daily. She went to bed every night re-living the decisions she had made throughout her day.

A year later, Pauline got married, quit her job, and went on to have a family. All throughout this transition in her life, she continued to worry, first about her homemaking abilities, then about the children, their health, their grades, whether they would get into a good college…and this was when they were toddlers. Worrying became a way of life for Pauline and it started to affect her health. She had no energy, felt stressed, kept getting sick with colds, wasn't sleeping well, and was beginning to gain weight. She complained of gastro-intestinal bloating and discomfort. After a series of medical tests she was diagnosed with IBS (irritable bowel syndrome). IBS differs from other types of intestinal disorders in that it may not be associated with inflammation but it is often related to stress.

THE MIND-BODY CONNECTION

The mind/body connection has been a tenet in Eastern medicine for thousands of years.

Many physicians who practice western medicine, also known as allopathic medicine, recognize the link between stress and illness as well.

In Chinese medicine, emotions are connected to specific energetic channels that, in turn, affect their corresponding organ. As an Acupuncturist I have treated many patients who, like Pauline, suffered from similar digestive imbalances. The relationship between worrying and the gastro-intestinal system is based on an imbalance of certain energetic channels that have connections with emotions, thoughts, and specific body systems. The system associated with worry is the Spleen/Stomach (SP/ST) "meridians" also known as "channels." Excessive worry weakens that system and may cause a flare-up of various symptoms. The SP/ST meridians are affected by other channels, one of them being the Liver meridian, which, when out of balance, may manifest as anger, frustration, and impatience. Stress, an unhealthy diet, unrestful or insufficient sleep, and poor interpersonal relationships are just some of the ways that meridians become unbalanced and may lead to illnesses.

Gastro-intestinal issues are commonly seen in people who worry excessively but they are, by far, not the only symptoms that are triggered by it. When you worry too much, your body may react the same way it would as if an emergency situation were to occur except that it is taking place over a longer period of time. Excess worrying is debilitating. It uses a lot of energy and eventually you run the risk of becoming more susceptible to a weakened immune system. We are all born with strengths and weaknesses and, depending on your particular constitution, your health can be affected in various ways.

Part of Pauline's treatment included a thorough psychological evaluation. In that process she came to realize that her chronic worrying was a habit. She had always associated habits with a physical behavior such as bingeing, smoking, exercise, and addictions, never thinking that habits could be of a mental nature.

Pauline is among many who worry. An article titled "Worried You're Not Alone" by Roni Caryn Rabin [32] reported that two of five Americans worry every day, according to a new paper released by Liberty Mutual Insurance.

When a worrisome thought pops up in your mind ask yourself:

1. Is this a real problem that is happening now or will happen in the near future?
2. How likely is this outcome to occur?
3. What is the worst that could happen?

4. Is there any evidence that supports the outcome you are envisioning?

5. Do you have control of the issue you're worrying about?

To stop her worrying, Pauline followed the steps of the Triple A's for Body, Mind, and Spirit.

First she became **aware** of her habit.

Then she took **action steps** by evaluating several methods for changing the habit. Luckily, her therapist was well versed with several effective methods for changing habits. (Chapter Three covers the most prevalent methods to date.) Pauline studied them carefully and decided to use Outcome Visioning developed by Dave Sellars, PhD. She also asked her brother-in-law to be her **accountability** partner. She had a good relationship with him and often turned to him for advice. In addition to the Outcome Visioning, Pauline kept a journal where she noted when her worries arose and the precipitating event that led to her worrying. She discussed these with her accountability partner. Her worrying started to decrease gradually until it assumed an acceptable level. Eventually she gave up her accountability partner with the understanding that he would be available if needed again. Most importantly, she continued her journaling.

MULTITASKING

One of the most prevalent habits created by the mind, and predominantly expressed by females, is multitasking. I have heard it said that men don't have the gene for it. But it's really not genetic; it's an acquired behavior. I have come to believe that if taken too far multitasking can disrupt the nervous system. I think of it as an old-fashioned switchboard, where the wires crisscrossed and people were connected to the wrong parties.

As an operating room nurse functioning as the scrub nurse (today called a surgical assistant), your job is to anticipate the needs of the surgical team and literarily slap instruments in their hands the moment they need it. At the same time, your other hand and your eyes are preparing for the following step. This is multitasking at its highest level. Years later, when I ran my private practice of chiropractic and acupuncture, I found that my multitasking skill came in very handy. But one day, I was cooking a dish that required constant stirring and I felt frustrated because I was doing just one thing at a time. I almost couldn't bear it. That's when I became **aware** that I had fallen into a habit of multitasking and not doing so was making me anxious. I examined my behavior and questioned the need to multitask at all times. My **action** steps included taking up knitting again. I remembered how much I enjoyed it and how it helped me focus one stitch at a time. I used the Tiny Habits method and concentrated on one situation at a time: I would not multitask at home between the hours of 10 and 2. I kept a journal to identify situations that would derail me. I asked my husband to be my **accountability partner.** It took me a few months to "quiet" down and enjoy the peacefulness and satisfaction of completing one task at a time.

LAZINESS

Would it surprise you to know that laziness is a habit? Laziness is both a learned behavior and a habit. It is also contagious, just like yawning can be. You may have learned it from the people around you.

I'm not talking about the occasional spring fever that many of us experience when the body, mind, and spirit need time out to restore energy. Rather, I'm referring to day-to-day low productivity behavior when you don't feel like doing anything not because you're tired but because you're not in the mood and when you leave for tomorrow what you can do today. Procrastination can be a manifestation of fear of failure or success, and it is also a form of laziness. It's important to differentiate between laziness and chronic fatigue. Being tired all the time is not a sign of laziness. It may be a sign of an underlying health issues.

Like all habits, the lazy habit can be changed, but only if you are **aware** that you have it and you **want to change it.** Choose just one chore that you are not attending to because you don't feel like it and work on it **every day.** Remember that to create a habit you take tiny steps and **repeat** it until it becomes second nature.

My friend Elaine doesn't make her bed when she gets up in the morning or hang up her clothes at night. When she became aware of her lazy habit she decided to work on making her bed every morning after brushing her teeth. Her roommate was more than happy to be her account-ability partner. It took her 6 weeks before she realized that not only was she making her bed automatically after brushing her teeth, but she had also started to hang up her clothing at night.

∽

PUNCTUALITY

Elsie was an excellent nurse but she was consistently late. She had been called into numerous evaluation con-ferences and every time she promised she would change her ways. She tried and for a while she showed improve-ment. Often, someone in the nursing team would cover for her until she showed up on duty. Then one night she was on call for emergencies and by the time she arrived at the hospital another nurse had taken over. The emergency was a feverish 8 year-old child who needed an appendectomy and there was no time to waste or the boy might have died. Elsie was fired.

As a rule, lives are not in danger when we are not punctual but often relationships, trust, and respect are broken because of this bad habit.

What constitutes being on time varies from person to person and is closely related to organizational skills and time management. It is a skill that is usually learned in childhood. My dad used to say to me that being on time for an appointment is being late. He would say, "You have to be there earlier to be on time." Learning to be on time strengthens character early on. It is a sign of integrity, responsibility, and dependability. It teaches discipline and shows respect for other people's time. Being late can add stress to your life, endanger your professional career and jeopardize your personal relationships.

As with any habit you are trying to change, being **aware** that you are chronically late is the first step. A friend told me that the first time he became aware that he was always late was when he found out that his friends would tell him to meet them at the movies or at dinner one hour before they all convened. He was so embarrassed that it motivated him to change his lateness habit.

Action steps for adopting punctuality:

1. Plan your day by estimating how long it will take you to get ready (shower, dress, etc.) to leave your home and how long it will take you to get to your destination or do your chores. Write down how long you think it will take you and then do several practice runs by timing yourself. Note the difference between your estimate and the actual time and write it down. Teach this to your children early on.

2. Once you have an idea of how long it will take to be somewhere, practice the 30-minute rule, which is to give yourself an additional 30 minutes to prepare for unexpected delays. If you should get to your destination early, enjoy the downtime. Bring something to read or answer or delete emails while you wait.

3. Avoid overbooking yourself and resist the temptation of trying to squeeze one more thing in to your agenda.

4. Be organized by keeping track, on your phone, computer, or paper calendar, of your appointments, things to do, and how long it will take you to get there.

5. Prepare your wardrobe the day before and check that you have whatever you need—transit card, credit card or cash for transportation, gas in the car, and paper work—for your appointment.

6. Mentally review your next day agenda.

7. Set your watch 5-10 minutes ahead.

Should you do all of these tips at the same time? Of course not. Simply choose one behavior at a time and practice it over and over again until it comes automatically. Then move on to the next plan. I have found that to incorporate a new habit in your life the Mantra Habit is very useful, for example: "I will be on time to meet my friends at the movies." Remember to emphasize a different word of the sentence every time. Take baby steps by committing yourself to one day of the week when you will be on time. Gradually increase the days.

Finally, be **accountable** to someone until punctuality is a habit.

THERE IS ALWAYS AVERSION THERAPY (BUT I DON'T RECOMMEND IT)

"A Shocking Way (Really) to Break Bad Habits" by Jennifer Jolly [33] is about getting rid of habits using a device called the Pavlok that provides an electric shock. The device was used to lose weight, to stop smoking, and to get out of bed every morning. It worked in every case.

It reminded me of a technique called aversion therapy or counter conditioning. Aversion therapy was originally developed to treat alcoholism. Eventually it became popular with other kinds of drug addictions, both street and prescription-related. I tried it many years ago when I was asked to participate in a study using aversion therapy to quit smoking. There were four of us, working in a hospital in various capacities. When I heard that volunteers were needed I jumped at the opportunity.

Here's how they set us up: The four of us sat side-by-side in back of a long table. There was an ashtray and a box of tissues on the table, and we were asked to put our packs of cigarettes next to these items. We each had a bucket on the right side of our chair. We didn't know why but after about one hour of chain smoking we figured it out. The researchers filmed us. We were not allowed to stop smoking but we had the option to raise our hands to leave the study if needed. I was the third one to quit. I stopped vomiting within an hour after I quit but remained nauseous for several days and didn't smoke for about two weeks after that ordeal. And then I encountered a particularly stressful event and by the end of the day I had bought a pack of cigarettes and was smoking again.

In aversion therapy, the person is exposed to an unpleasant stimulus in conjunction with a behavior they are trying to get rid of. In the smoking cessation experiment that I participated in, the sick feeling that I felt from smoking one cigarette after another should have turned me off from smoking, and it did. But, without reinforcement, the old habit was quick to re-emerge.

When it comes to changing habits it's important to keep in mind that habits never really disappear. Still, you can definitely change them by selecting one of the many techniques available and sticking to it until the new behavior itself becomes a habit.

CHAPTER FIVE:

The Habits of Health

The sign on the staff lounge of the operating room where I worked read: Smoking permitted in this area. That was in the mid 70's, around the time when the Surgeon General first released the statement that smoking was bad for our health. Those were the days when doctors smoked while treating patients and when patients could smoke in their hospital rooms even if they were not private rooms. I don't remember exactly when the sign was removed but it must have been before 1993 when the Joint Commission on Accreditation of Health Care Organizations (JCAHO) banned smoking in hospital buildings.

Our nation has come a long way from those smoke-filled days. Unfortunately, other habits developed that have led to obesity, which has the distinct dishonor of being the #1 epidemic in the U.S.

But obesity is not the only epidemic that plagues our society. Sleep dysfunction, drug addiction, sedentary lifestyles, habits that can lead to violent behavior, such as watching violent video games: these and many others contribute to a less than healthy population. They are mostly created by what is referred to as habits of disease.

The key to healthy habits is not a mystery to most Americans, and especially for those who live in big cities where there is an infinite amount of information in the form of meet-ups and classes offering information about nutrition, exercise, and stress reduction. Yet, the health of Americans compared to those in other developed nations is not good.

Upon a request initiated by the National Institutes of Health (NIH), the National Research Council and the Institute of Medicine created a panel to discuss the health issues of America and its implications. This culminated in a report in 2013 titled "U.S. Health in International Perspective: Shorter Lives, Poorer Health." [34] The committee compared the health status of the U.S. with statistics from 16 peer countries of comparable high-income democracies in Western Europe, along with Canada, Australia, and Japan.

They concluded that Americans fared worse in at least nine areas of health: infant mortality and low birth weight, injuries and homicides, adolescent pregnancy and sexually transmitted infections, HIV and AIDS, drug-related deaths, obesity and diabetes, heart disease, chronic lung disease, and disability. They went on to say that "The U.S. health disadvantage cannot be attributed solely to the adverse health status of racial or ethnic minorities or poor people: even highly advantaged Americans are in worse health than their counterparts in other 'peer' countries."

The real problem is not ignorance; it's non-compliance. The question is WHY? What is driving this behavior? Why is there non-compliance? Could negative habits be a source of culpability?

To counteract those negative habits, this chapter will cover the healthy habits of:

✓ Posture

✓ Sleep

✓ Motion

✓ Mind

The healthy habits of eating are covered in the following chapter.

You'll see how each of these healthy habits interacts with each other, integrating body, mind, and spirit.

THE HABIT OF HEALTHY POSTURE

A healthy posture is one that preserves the natural curves of our body and places the least amount of strain on the supporting soft tissues and joints. I like to demonstrate proper posture to my patients as I instill a vision of them walking down an aisle, for instance to get the degree they worked so hard for or when they got married:

- ✓ Head straight and stretched upward with chin slightly inward but not down

- ✓ Earlobes in line with the shoulders

- ✓ Shoulder blades held gently back but not in military position

- ✓ Knees straight but not locked when standing

- ✓ Stomach tucked and pelvis in a neutral position, that is neither swaybacked nor hunched forward.

I have a habit of observing people's physical structure and gait as they walk ahead of me on the streets. This one's feet pronate (turn inward), that one's shoulder or hip is higher than the other. The head is tilted to the right on that man and the abnormal curvature in the woman's spine causes her head to face downward. I am also very conscious of their weight because that's what Chiropractors do.

My observations as an Acupuncturist are different. I watch people as they face me. Posture tells me a great deal about their Qi (energy.) I notice their eyes, complexion and hair and whether they are bright or dull or if there are dark circles under their eyes. Are they walking with vigor or dragging their feet or are they wobbling from side to side? Again, I am very conscious of their weight because that's what Acupuncturists do.

Healthy habits are written in our persona. You don't have to be a doctor to perceive that someone is not healthy. The challenge is being self-aware. If you could see yourself objectively, walking down the street, peeking a view of yourself at a store window or a mirror, what would you see? Be honest.

Mary was one of my favorite patients. She had come to my office for acupuncture to help with her wrist pain. I noticed right away her exquisite posture and complimented her on it. It is rare to see people nowadays with good posture. Mary told me that she was always aware of her posture because of a mild scoliosis that was discovered when she was 11 years-old during a routine check up in a new school. She was told that if it got worse she would need to wear a brace. She wanted to avoid it so badly that she made it her business to adopt a perfect standing posture from then on. A runaway scoliosis, one that progresses rapidly especially during growth spurts, may not respond to posture. In Mary's case, her scoliosis remained mild and it served her to become conscious of her posture. It broadened her awareness and mindfulness about her sitting and sleeping posture as well. She engaged the help of friends and family to point out to her when her posture was poor. (accountability) She peeked in many mirrors and store windows and even tied a string between the two straps of her bra in the back to keep her back straight. In time her excellent posture became a habit.

THE HABIT OF HEALTHY SLEEP

Insufficient sleep is a public health problem that, along with obesity, has reached epidemic proportions in the U.S., according to the Centers for Disease Control and Prevention (CDC). [35] More than a third of Americans are not getting their 7 or more hours of sleep on a regular basis. The link between not enough sleep and obesity can be attributed to poor habits such as decreased exercise, as well as hormonal imbalance associated with hunger and satiation.

Poor sleep interfaces with some of the major players that affect the health of our society, including hypertension [36], Type 2 diabetes, [37], and cardiovascular diseases [38.]

The effects of sleep deficit on our mental wellbeing are something most of us can relate to. When we don't get enough sleep we experience a variety of symptoms ranging from being foggy and irritable with difficulty focusing and concentrating, to being downright impossible to live with. Sometimes the outcome is even tragic.

My friend Ellen suffered from chronic insomnia. She was a researcher in a large medical center and had been taking sleep medications for years. Gradually, they stopped working. They also made her groggy during the day. Ingrained in Western science, she had no affinity for alternative healing methods but because we were friends she was considering using acupuncture and chiropractic. She put up with me when I told her about the benefits of these complementary approaches but she never started treatments. Ellen died in a car accident. She had fallen asleep at the wheel.

Together with family and friends, we mourned our loss and celebrated her life. A few months later, her husband called and asked if I would help dispense her belongings, as he was getting ready to move. While going through her closet I noticed a poster from the National Sleep Foundation [39] listing the established sleep hygiene tips to improve sleep:

✓ Stick to a sleep schedule **of the same bedtime and wake up time, even on the weekends.** This helps to regulate your body's clock and could help you fall asleep and stay asleep for the night.

✓ **Practice a relaxing bedtime ritual.** A relaxing, routine activity right before bedtime conducted away from bright lights helps separate your sleep time from activities that can cause excitement, stress or anxiety that can make it more difficult to fall asleep, get sound and deep sleep or remain asleep.

✓ **If you have trouble sleeping, avoid naps, especially in the afternoon.** Power napping may help you get through the day, but if you find that you can't fall asleep at bedtime, eliminating even short catnaps may help.

✓ **Exercise daily.** Vigorous exercise is best, but even light exercise is better than no activity. Exercise at any time of day but not at the expense of your sleep.

✓ **Evaluate your room.** Design your sleep environment to establish the conditions you need for sleep. Your bedroom should be cool, between 60 and 67 degrees. Your bedroom should also be free from any noise that can disturb your sleep. Finally, your bedroom should be free from any light. Check your room for noises or other distractions. This includes a bed partner's sleep disruptions such as snoring. Consider using blackout curtains, eyeshades, earplugs, "white noise" machines, humidifiers, fans and other devices.

✓ **<u>Sleep on a comfortable mattress and pillows.</u>** Make sure your mattress is comfortable and supportive. The one you have been using for years may have exceeded its life expectancy—about 9 or 10 years for most good quality mattresses. Use comfortable pillows and make the room attractive and inviting for sleep but also free of <u>allergens </u>that might affect you and objects that might cause you to slip or fall if you have to get up.

I stared at the poster for I don't know how long. I remember thinking over and over again, "what good is it to know the right things to do if you don't implement them?" And then I realized it: Ellen was aware of her problem but she couldn't take action steps because she didn't have the tools to help her change her habits. Nobody told her to focus on one recommendation at a time or to be accountable to someone for each new step.

~⌇~

HEALTHY MOTION

Show me a room full of exercise machines and I will run away. Give me a Zumba class or even just earphones, my music, and a mirror and I'm on for an hour of crazy dancing. That's just me. What turns you on to moving your body, elevate your spirit, and calm your mind? If you love your workout you stand a better chance to make it a habit and that's what you want to do.

I never thought I'd be enjoying all the walking and stair climbing I do almost every day in Manhattan. What a perk it is to get healthy motion in daily living. The street is my treadmill and the stairways my Stairmaster. I also take advantage of household chores and practice squats when I empty the garbage and pick up things from the floor. When I reach for the upper shelves of my cupboard I do it with the intention of stretching. I even use public transportation for subtle gentle stretches as I hold on to the top straps or the poles while alternating going on my toes and heels. I love walking Bo and Bella, my four-legged babies because I get to do more squats when I pick up their poop. At my desk, I get up frequently and walk around the apartment, mingling some housework in-between my work at the computer.

There aren't enough adjectives that I can list as benefits of physical activity. You may not lose weight with exercise but it will help maintain a healthy weight plus a whole lot more.

Exercise strengthens the muscles in the body and the heart and decreases the risk of cardiovascular disease. Studies have shown that physical activity can improve high blood pressure and help prevent and manage many health problems including high blood pressure, stroke, Type 2 diabetes, and certain types of cancer. It strengthens your muscles, improves flexibility, endurance and balance, and helps keep joints healthy. It increases energy, but also induces a sense of relaxation. It puts you in a better mood, promotes good sleep, improves brain function, increases circulation and brings on better sex.

Exercise makes you feel good in body and mind, and the spirit is lifted when you put in a good workout. There is nothing automatic about the exercise itself. The habit is in making it a part of your life.

If you are already reaping the benefits of exercise, hurray for you! If, on the other hand, you're not presently physically active, "know before you go." That means find out what works best for you by experimenting with a variety of exercises and find the one that brings you the most sweat, happiness, fun or whatever other meaning it brings to your life. Now make it a habit by repeating it, repeating it, and repeating it until it becomes automatic.

There is no need to buy expensive equipment or a workout wardrobe, but a pair of good sneakers is essential not just to do the exercise but also to serve as a cue. Put them near your bed so that they motivate you to start a routine. Seeing the sneakers gets your brain and body habituated to exercise, even if you decide to do yoga, which doesn't require sneakers. Once the sight of the shoes causes an automatic reaction to exercise you will not no longer need the cue, but you may still need the sneakers.

And keep in mind that an exercise buddy is a great source of motivation to keep the habit going.

My friend Jenny was getting married in the fall. Her fiancée, Gregg, was a runner and Jenny had promised him that she would start running again with him once they were married so they could enjoy the experience together and keep each other accountable. She had been a runner in college but fell out of the habit once she moved out of the city to live in the suburbs. She found it difficult to get back into the habit. She'd get up early to commute to Manhattan and came home too late to do anything other than grab a quick bite, take a bath, read and go to sleep.

How was Jenny going to get back to her old habit of running? Her goal was to exercise in the morning before going to work. That required that she get up even earlier. To start, Jenny planned to do a short run around the block one day a week. She started on a Sunday when she wouldn't be pressured for time and then eased herself into the tighter schedule for the weekdays. She looked for a whole bunch of pictures that she had of herself when she was in the running team in college and posted them on a 'dream' board in full view on her hall table. She bought herself a new pair of sneakers and placed them by the side of her bed even on days that she wasn't running. She monitored herself by keeping track of her running and how she felt during and after the run. Before going to sleep every night she used the Mantra Habit, which was: "I am grateful to be running again."

Her reward was a deep sense of satisfaction knowing that she was on her way to her old habit. Gregg was her accountability partner. Once she started to run automatically she gradually increased her time and then she steadily increased the days of the week that she'd run. It took Jenny 6 weeks to get back to her old running habit.

HEALTHY MIND

A healthy mind is one that is in balance with busyness and quiet. Finding that quiet time is the challenge most Americans face. Meditation is the ultimate form of quieting the mind and for some people it comes easily. Many people struggle with it. I once did a survey and asked all my patients if they practiced any type of meditation. Very few said they did. Getting into the habit of meditating daily requires determination and perseverance. There are many resources available to help people who are seriously interested in pursuing this form of quieting the mind.

I had a patient who tried many times to learn meditation. She attended lectures, read books, listened to CD's and apps on her phone, and even had private sessions with a meditation teacher. All this was before she sought acupuncture for stress reduction. The acupuncture that I practice is mostly done on the extremities, with all my patients seated on a recliner. I encourage my patients to bring their earphones and provide them with relaxing music while they are being treated. My patient learned that she could find quiet time without meditation by listening to music, reading, writing in her diary, or taking a relaxing bath with essential oils. Most importantly, she made it a habit of scheduling her quiet time every day in her calendar.

ONE GOOD HABIT CAN START ANOTHER

In the Introduction I made reference to keystone habits as core habits that empower other behaviors to be tagged along. Keystone habits are especially important when we focus on habits of health: healthy weight, eating, motion, sleep, and mind. As a health coach, I have found that once clients start to see significant results in their weight loss they are motivated to explore other health benefits such as exercise, better sleep habits, and effective stress reduction techniques. This is what a keystone habit does. It propels a series of chain reactions that produce positive outcomes. That is what happened with Janet, one of my clients.

Janet called me to see if I could help her lose weight. She had gained about 30 lbs. since she lost her job a few months before. She was writing her second mystery novel and had no time to exercise. She felt a lot of pressure to work on her book and as a result she slept poorly and felt very stressed. Soon after she started the program and lost her first 10 lbs. she started Pilates classes on her own. A few months later, she shared with me that her sleep had become more restorative than ever. The combination of all these 'small wins' provided her with a sense of relaxation she had not experienced in years. Her stress levels were greatly reduced and her writing flourished.

No one ever said it was easy to change habits of disease to habits of health. The only time it is easier is when those habits actually turn into disease. Given a diagnosis that threatens your life can turn your mind 180 degrees toward making habit changes. Why wait when you can feel better now?

CHAPTER SIX:

———◇◆◇———

The Habit of Healthy Eating and Reaching a Healthy Weight

Several years ago, I treated a patient for low back pain when she was pregnant. Since I was a delivery room nurse at one time, I enjoyed treating pregnant women and was just as excited about her pregnancy as she was. Soon after her baby girl was born she moved to Florida, and I lost track of her. One day, she called me. We chatted for a while and then she told me the bad news: her baby was born with the Prader-Willi syndrome (PWS), a complex and rare genetic disorder that occurs in about 15,000 live births. The most common genetic cause of obesity, it is characterized by general abnormal developmental features including musculo-skeletal weakness, physical growth retardation, lowered metabolism and a ravenous appetite that is never satiated. Areas where food is available must be under lock and key at all times.

PWS is differentially diagnosed from other genetic disorders that cause obesity such as Bardet-Biedl syndrome which, in addition to obesity, affects many parts of the body such as vision, extra fingers or toes (polydactyly), learning disabilities and abnormalities of the genitalia to name a few.

$$\smile$$

GENETICS VS. ENVIRONMENT

In addition to these rare genetic variations of syndromes that cause obesity there are other genetic predispositions and mutations that lead to obesity and that run in families. The obesity epidemic seen in the US and globally is the combination of these genetic variations and an obesogenic environment. Jason M. Satterfield, PhD, is a Professor of Clinical Medicine University of California, San Francisco, and teaches a course titled *Mind-Body Medicine: The New Science of Optimal Health*. Dr. Satterfield states that studies have shown that the contribution to obesity from genetics is somewhere between 25 and 40%. He goes on to state that, "The Institute of Medicine and the World Health Organization conclude that although genetics is important, the environment is the largest single influence on body weight." [40].

What exactly is an obesogenic environment? In short, it is an environment that promotes weight gain through unhealthy food choices and discourages physical activity. The study of obesity is extensive and on going and it is very dear to my heart. My specialty in the field of health coaching is closely related to the obesity epidemic and the decline of healthy habits leading to optimal health. It is not within the scope of this book to discuss all the issues related to obesity other than what are the habits that lead to obesity and, more importantly, what are the habits to adopt that lead us away from obesity. These can only be examined through the lenses of the environment. Today's food choices are not only unhealthy in content and quality but also in quantity. The portions of every kind of most foods and beverages have increased at a range of 20 to 60% in the past 20 years. Along with this increase in quantity there is an equal increase in empty calories. The average restaurant meal is four times larger than it was in the 1950s.

Lack of physical activity stands right alongside with poor eating habits as a big part of the obesity epidemic. The impact of technology on lifestyle has caused a dramatic reduction of everyday activities that kept our energy expenditure in balance with out energy intake.

There are those who believe that significant weight loss can be achieved mostly with exercise and those who believe that diet takes precedence. Most authorities on the subject lean toward diet as the primary means to lose weight and exercise to maintain the weight loss. In my own practice as a health coach and a physical fitness instructor,

I recommend that patients begin their health journey by first addressing their diet. The reasons for that are threefold. First, it can be dangerous to exercise when you are very overweight as you could injure your joints, especially your knees and low back, and particularly if you haven't been exercising regularly. Second, many of my clients who tried to lose weight through exercise alone were unsuccessful in the long run because their appetite increased after exercising, and they had the mindset that they could eat heartily since they had burned calories already. Third, most of my clients reported that once they started to lose weight, even if just a few pounds, their body felt lighter and they felt a natural desire to move more which gradually led them to exercise regularly on their own.

The overwhelming majority of the studies I have reviewed over the years revealed that a combination of diet and exercise is the most effective way to lose weight. However, starting both at the same time can be a bit too much to undertake. Making one change at a time and reinforcing it regularly is a better way to ensure that a habit will be formed.

There is no shortage of information about nutrition, fitness and wellness. You can read it in books, magazines and online; you can watch it on TV and videos, you can listen to it on the radio and attend any number of lectures easily available in a myriad of venues. The information is there for anyone who is truly interested in educating himself or herself about how to optimize his or her health.

However, as I see it, there are three problems related to health habits. One is that people are often stuck in their habits and they don't know how to change them. The second is that people are busy with other concerns and don't pay attention to their unhealthy habits until they become sick. The third is that people are in denial of their bad habits.

Following a presentation that I gave about obesity as a risk factor for breast cancer, a woman who was considerably overweight approached me and said, "I know what I have to do to lose weight but I just can't seem to get started." I hear many people say that. It sounds so powerless, like they are being controlled by their habits. But until they make a decision to change they will always be slaves to them.

For instance, years ago I had been treating Jack off and on for chronic low back pain with chiropractic and acupuncture. Every time he came to the office he was in agony and couldn't stand up straight. Once or twice I had to make a house call because he was in too much pain to come to the office. If it wasn't his back it was his knees. He'd get better with the treatments only to return a few months later with another attack. Jack was 5' 8" and weighed 259 lbs. "You need to lose weight," I kept telling him. "I know Dr.

Heyman," he'd answer me. "I'll start my diet tomorrow and go to the gym as soon as I feel better." But he never did.

And, I admit, I did not guide him well. I didn't even know myself at the time that diet alone, without someone to support him throughout his journey, would probably not work. I learned much later how important it is for people to avail themselves of a support system and surround themselves with like-minded people for long-term success. It isn't enough for doctors to tell their patients that they need to lose weight. Doctors must take a more active part in helping patients find programs that provide weight-loss and habit-forming strategies as well as support through their journey. Nutritionists and dietitians are excellent sources of dietary education and health coaches provide the much-needed support, accountability and reinforcement that is essential for lifestyle changes.

Health and wellness programs for health coaching offer a different approach to helping people create optimal health in their lives. What these programs teach is the support and accountability that many people need to get started on their path to optimal health. A key element to this approach is understanding the role of habits in behaviors that lead to unhealthy life styles.

TAKE ANOTHER LOOK

In Chapter Three there is an outline of a series of methods for adopting new habits and changing unwanted ones. In addition to the Mantra Habit, my own creation, they are:

1. The Framework by Charles Duhigg using the Habit Loop idea

2. Microresolutions by Caroline Arnold

3. Tiny Habits/The Fogg method created by B.J. Fogg, PhD

4. Smart Change by Art Markman, PhD

5. Stop or Start Habits/Outcome Visioning by Dave Sellars, PhD

6. The Little Book of Change by Amy Johnson, PhD

You can change most of your unhealthy habits with any of these methods. Choose the method that suits you best at a particular time and for a specific habit.

However, there are two additional methods that are particularly suitable to change eating habits that lead to obesity.

One is called the Stop Challenge Choose method, created by Dr. Wayne Scott Andersen, author of Dr. A's *Habits of Health* and *Discover Your Optimal Health: The Guide to Taking Control of Your Weight, Your Vitality, Your Life*. [41] The other is a method called W.A.I.T. which stands for 'What

Am I Thinking?' created by Wendy Hendry, a health coach and author of *W.A.I.T. loss: The Keys to Food Freedom and Winning the Battle of the Binge.* [42]

STOP CHALLENGE CHOOSE

The Stop Challenge Choose option worked really well for Bernadette, one of my clients. Here is her story.

"I've been struggling with weight since I was a teenager," she began. "Throughout my adult life I've been on countless diets, none of which worked long term. I would lose weight and gradually put it on again. I knew that this yo-yoing was not healthy and could actually work against me. I've read that the hypothalamus is a part of the brain that sends messages to the body through many chemicals, telling it whether it should gain or lose weight and the body responds to these signals by adjusting hunger, activity, and metabolism to keep the weight stable."

And indeed, Bernadette was right. According to neuroscientist Dr. Sandra Aamodt, our brain has its own sense of what we should weigh. "Metabolic suppression," she states, "is one of several powerful tools that the brain uses to keep the body within a certain weight range, called the set point." This set point, which is determined by genes and life experience, varies from person to person. Dr. Aamodt stresses the point that when someone is dieting and their weight drops below that set point, "they not only burn fewer calories but also produce more hunger-inducing hormones and find eating more rewarding." [43]

Bernadette realized that her lifestyle was robbing her from leading a healthy life but didn't know how to change it. She wanted to learn to make healthy food choices, especially when socializing at dinner parties. She shared with me that she desperately wanted to exercise regularly but just couldn't muster any motivation. She also yearned for better sleep without having to use her C-pack for sleep apnea. (The C-pack is a device used when a person is sleeping in order to avoid periods of non-breathing.) She blamed herself for not having enough willpower and that brought a great deal of stress in her life.

"At my last physical examination," Bernadette told me, "my doctor said that my blood pressure was elevated and that I was a borderline diabetic." I'm 45 years old and scared that I will end up like my mother who died of a heart attack at age 50."

I asked Bernadette if she was ready to make a change in her life, reminding her that all change requires a certain kind of commitment. When she said that she was, I gave her a self-assessment designed by Drs. Prochaska, Norcross, and DeClemente (see page 54.) I wanted to make sure that both of us knew what stage of change she was in. From our conversation I thought she might be in the Preparation stage (intention to change within the next 30 days), which was confirmed by her answers to the self-assessment. In addition, I asked her many questions including what was the main reason that she wanted to lose weight. How did her weight affect her daily life, for instance walking and exercising? How did it affect her social life and relation-ships? What was Bernadette hoping to change when she reached her healthy weight?

We discussed Bernadette's eating habits, sleeping rou-tine, and stress level as well. It was obvious that many poor habits were contributing to her obesity. I put her on a program that would help Bernadette reach her healthy weight and learn the habits of health for long-term success. I provided her with information on joining a community of like-minded people for additional support and guidance. "Doing all these things," I told her, "will help you achieve your goals for a healthy body, mind, and spirit."

I explained to Bernadette that at first these actions would require the prefrontal brain to work. But in time, as this behavior is repeated over and over again, it will become a habit, which will serve her on other challenging occasions.

I reminded her that it's not unusual for family and friends to sabotage a person's best intentions to stay on plan by en-couraging them to indulge. "Oh, go on, it's only one day of the year" they might say. "If you are mentally prepared for what you expect might occur you will be able to elicit their cooperation to help you through your health goals. You might even want to tell your family and friends ahead of time that you are on a health program and you would appreciate their help not to tempt you to indulge. This will be easier to implement if you have already lost weight and people are commenting on it."

Bernadette embraced the program I recommended. This is what she said to me: "I want to participate in the whole program because I know that diet alone is not enough. I want to change my habits and create healthy ones."

The program that Bernadette started included meal replacements. Studies have shown that meal replacements or plans that provided meals were the most successful for weight loss. The program was perfect for Bernadette's lifestyle, as she explained. [44]

"It's very important to me that the program is easy to implement and requires very little decision making. As the chief financial officer of a large corporation, I make many important decisions in the course of the day. By the evening, when I get home from work, my brain is fried and my willpower is totally depleted."

As she began to lose weight her motivation to exercise increased. Once her new eating system had become second nature, she was ready to make changes in the other areas of her life. The structured eating plan had become a keystone habit that lead to starting an exercise program and a better sleep routine.

"In the past," recounted Bernadette, "I would starve myself so I could eat all the calories I saved during the day. The next day I would feel bloated and angry for overeating. Now I do things differently.

"First, I visualize my goals. How much weight do I want to lose and why? What size pants do I want to get into? What size dress do I plan on buying in the near future? What will I be able to do once I reach my goal?

Next, I right my goals down.

"Then, before going to an event, I have my usual meal replacements every 2-3 hours, making sure that the last one is eaten shortly before the party. When I arrive, I do my 'fake' drinking by holding a glass of water with a slice of lime. Then, I take a bird's eye view of the table and when I come upon a dish that I am interested in having, instead of reaching out automatically for it I STOP. I CHALLENGE myself by questioning whether this choice would take me closer or further away from my goals, and then I make a decision. Sometimes I pass up that particular dish altogether and other times I CHOOSE to just have a tablespoon and move on.

"With this method, I was able to go through the end of year holidays without gaining one pound. The Stop Challenge Choose method is like a mantra that gives me the time to think, be aware, and be mindful of what I'm doing. I also use this mantra for many other situations. I've used it when I get annoyed with someone and before I say something I may regret. I also employ it when shopping— for smaller clothes!"

OVERCOME BINGEING WITH THE W.A.I.T. AND CLICK APPROACH

Wendy Hendry's method is specifically designed to overcome bingeing. It is a fairly simple technique, which makes it easy to execute.

All you will need is an index card—this is your Awareness Card that you will use as a reminder to stop and "hear" the thoughts coming from your brain—and some kind of a tracker such as the ones in knitting stores to track stitches. She calls this device the "Craving Tracker."

The routine is to write W.A.I.T. on the front of an index card. Below, write your Higher Level "why" which is the driving force behind your motivation.

On the back of your Awareness Card, write "Time and Trigger, " "Acknowledge" and "Ignore."

You'll want to keep the card in a place where you can see it often. When you want to eat, stop and ask yourself, "What Am I Thinking?" If you are headed into the kitchen to binge, ask yourself whether you are feeling hunger or a craving. If it is a craving, try to identify the trigger. Write it in the "Trigger" column. Take a second to acknowledge the craving: "Yes, urge, I hear you." Mark the "Acknowledgment" column with an X. If you ignore the craving, mark it with an X. The last step is the reward: If you ignored the urge, give yourself a click on your Cravings Tracker.

THE HABIT OF HEALTHY EATING

Healthy eating is more than just what you eat; it is also about why, how, and when you eat. These are the four components that comprise healthy eating. What you eat is about the value of your food. Some people already know the basics of good nutrition, that is, lean protein, veggies, fruits, whole grains, healthy fats, low-fat dairy and lots of water. However, in our society, there are plenty of controversial issues regarding what constitutes a healthy diet. At one time, fat was the great evil and foods like eggs and avocados were considered poor choices for people who needed to curtail their cholesterol. Today, healthy fats are in and sugar is considered the culprit for many of the chronic inflammatory diseases that plague our society. The guidelines keep changing. Therefore, this chapter is not about diet or nutrition. Rather, it is about habits of eating that contribute to the obesity epidemic and those habits can be changed.

(Some medications and hormonal imbalances can contribute to weight gain. It's important to keep an eye on your weight over time and notice any unusual changes. Be sure to check with your physician before beginning any kind of weight reduction plan.)

EVERYONE EATS DIFFERENTLY

We eat for sustenance but we also eat because it is an enjoyable experience and often one that is associated with socializing. Whatever the reasons, eating habits can often spin out of control.

Mandy's aunt, who had lost a lot of weight and was leading a new lifestyle since she started an optimal health program, referred her niece to me. "I know I'm overweight Dr. Heyman and I don't understand why," Mandy said when we first met. " I don't have a sweet tooth and, in fact, I dislike chocolate. I never eat cake, cookies, ice cream, or candy. The only sweet food I enjoy is fruit, and I eat plenty of them. My Achilles's heel is salty food, but I'm careful about that also. I pretty much eat healthy, so I don't understand why my weight keeps creeping up." At my urging, she went on to tell me what her days were like in terms of her eating. I asked her to tell me what and how much she ate, and how she ate, whether alone or not, sitting or standing, and what she did while eating. I had a suspicion that her problem wasn't what she ate but how she ate it. This is her story:

"I begin my day with breakfast, a bowl of cereal with some kind of fruit, usually a banana, and a slice of whole grain bread with a cup of tea. I eat standing at the kitchen counter while checking my schedule for the day. Sometimes I skim through the newspaper. Lunch and dinner are always with friends, colleagues, or family. I am fanatical about avoiding junk food, and although I love potato chips because they are crunchy and salty, you will never see as much as one in my home. I'm sure that I would pass the test from any nutritionist about the quality of food I eat. Why then am I overweight?" she asked again, this time with a greater sense of exasperation.

"Well," I said to her, "if the quality of your food is good then let's take a look at the other aspects of eating such as how much you eat and what goes on in your environment while you eat." She went on to share the following:

"Most of the time, I eat a large salad with lots of healthy veggies and either chicken or turkey for lunch. In the afternoon I have a bowl of fruit or cut up veggies and in the evening I have a large plate of some kind of protein, chicken or turkey mostly, sometimes lean ham, with lots of veggies and a baked potato, brown rice or quinoa. About one hour before going to bed I like to munch on all kinds of nuts. I also keep nuts in my office for an afternoon snack."

Mandy admitted that she ate fast and although she loved her food she wasn't very mindful about eating. "When I eat alone," she said, "I'm usually doing something else like reading a magazine or talking on the phone. When I eat with someone else I enjoy my conversations and often I keep eating even when I feel full."

I asked Mandy if she ever ate for other reasons besides hunger, for instance when she was upset. "Yes," she said. "I often eat when I'm frustrated, bored, and anxious, especially when I'm moody around the time of my period." I pointed out to Mandy that it's important to be aware of the brain/gut interaction warning her that she's had enough and that eating slowly and mindfully encourages that awareness. We discussed other issues surrounding her eating patterns and I asked her to put together a list of the things that she wanted to change. That list would help Mandy's awareness that food alone was not the reason she was steadily gaining weight.

Let's analyze Mandy's eating habits in terms of the what, how, why and when:

<u>What:</u> Mandy eats healthy food only.

How: Mandy eats mindlessly and excessively.

Why: Mandy eats for many reasons: because she is hungry, because she likes to eat, and oftentimes for emotional reasons.

When: Mandy eats three large meals a day and snacks in-between meals.

Mandy was overweight not because she ate the wrong foods but because of unhealthy eating habits. She was at risk of becoming obese if she continued on this path. Realizing that she needed to change her eating patterns, she was ready to start a program that would help her lose weight and learn the habits leading to a healthier life.

⌒⌒

CONTRAST MANDY'S HABITS WITH CINDY'S

Her internist referred Cindy to me not because she was overweight, but because he thought she needed a health coach to teach her a healthier lifestyle. She had come to him with a chief complaint of chronic fatigue and not having enough energy to exercise. After a thorough examination and blood work he told her she was anemic. He recommended some iron pills and sent her to me.

Cindy is married and raised three children who are all adults and out of the house. When we first met, I asked

Cindy to tell me about herself and her health goals.

"I never liked cooking," she confessed. "I raised my kids pretty much the way I was brought up, with a lot of love but very little structure, especially in regards to meals. Dinner was often fast food—pizza, Mexican, or Burger King--and the leftovers were served the next night. From the time I was a 7 year-old, I fixed my own breakfast, usually cereal, and sometimes skipped it altogether. I often missed eating lunch and on days when I wasn't in school I sometimes warmed up the leftover restaurant food.

"My husband works in a local diner and we eat most of our meals there. I am a real estate broker and my schedule is very erratic. I don't think too much about eating and, I must admit, I don't have too many nutritious foods in my cupboard. I do keep some snacks around in case we get hungry and want something to nibble on. Sometimes I go a whole day without eating and when I finally get hungry, I eat whatever is around while checking my email and texts."

Let's analyze Cindy's eating habits in terms of her what, how, and why and when:

<u>What</u>: Cindy's food choices are unhealthy.

<u>How</u>: Cindy eats mindlessly and quickly.

<u>Why</u>: Cindy eats just to satisfy hunger.

<u>When</u>: Cindy has no set time for meals.

Cindy is not overweight but her eating habits are not healthy and already beginning to show in her health status.

A striking commonality between Mandy and Cindy is their lack of mindfulness when eating. The fact that they both consulted with me showed that there was already a certain degree of awareness regarding their health. Mandy sought help because she was gradually gaining more weight and that concerned her. Cindy was not feeling well and was open to her doctor's recommendation to speak to a health coach. They were both ready to make a change in their lives. My job was to take them from a state of awareness to a state of heightened awareness.

I asked each to write their present reality on the bottom of a 5x8 sheet of paper. On the top, I told them to write down the change they wanted to achieve. Eventually they would fill in the **action** steps they would need to take to reach each goal. Alongside the action steps I instructed them to fill out a goals date. They were to do this in baby steps, that is, one small action at a time. I offered myself as an **accountability** partner or they could seek someone else if they preferred.

In addition, I asked them to come up with a centering thought that they would repeat throughout the exercise.

Lastly, I asked them to create a **Mantra Habit** that would sustain them throughout their journey.

I also provided them with guidelines and tips for healthy eating: My basic recommendations for healthy eating habits included the following:

1. Eat breakfast within the first two hours of awakening.

2. Eat small nutritious meals every 3 hours to keep blood sugar and insulin levels balanced.

3. Keep the portions small. One way of keeping a check on portions is to use a 9-inch plate. Another way is to allocate a certain amount for snacking. For instance, 12 nuts are better than a bagful.

4. Chew your food thoroughly for healthy digestion and slowly and mindfully for the full enjoyment.

5. Drink plenty of water throughout the day.

6. Be mindful and in touch with your body and the signals it sends you when you are eating. Are you eating because you are hungry or to satisfy an emotional need? Ask yourself when you ate last. If it was less than an hour ago and you are thinking about food look further into your mood. What is really drawing you to food?

I also recommended a mindful meditation that I'm particularly fond of. It goes like this: Place one raisin in your mouth. Focus on the texture, the taste, and the size of the raisin. Swish the raisin around your mouth but make sure you don't bite into it. Instead, run your tongue around it and capture the sensation that it brings you. Notice how the raisin's texture becomes smoother and smoother, the taste sweeter and sweeter, and the size becomes smaller and smaller until the raisin is completely absorbed.

Many of my patients find this mindful meditation easy to do, and as a result they are more receptive and able to make a habit of using it.

IMPLEMENT THESE RECOMMENDATIONS UNTIL THEY BECOME HABITUAL

To create healthy eating habits in your daily life begin by choosing one area that you would like to work on first. For Mandy, it was enjoying breakfast while sitting down at her dining room table and eating it slowly without checking her schedule or doing anything else. Mandy incorporated the Mantra Habit just before sitting down to eat her breakfast with the following: 'I am enjoying every bite of my breakfast in peace and calm' and she checked in with me once a week. What she discovered after instituting her new routine was that she naturally became more mindful of her eating experience. She recognized when she felt satiated and ate less food. Gradually Mandy took on more areas that she wanted to change as she became comfortable and used to her new habit. Next, Mandy tackled her portion control. It was easier now that she was more mindful and alert to being full. One small change— sitting at the table to eat breakfast without distraction—brought on a series of small wins. By becoming more mindful and eating less food, Mandy lost 40 lbs. over a period of 4 months. She was on her way to better health.

Cindy began her journey to better habits by stocking nutritious foods in her kitchen instead of the junk food that was available in the past. She shopped once a week and had little difficulty reaching out for those foods. However, the next step was to eat more regularly. That was more challenging for her. She scheduled one day of the week to eat breakfast, lunch, and dinner at designated times. The rest of the week she could eat whenever she wanted. It wasn't long before she started to eat regularly all the time. Cindy's energy started to improve gradually and took a quantum leap when she started to eat on a regular basis. "I feel transformed," she told me. "I even started exercising and I love the way I feel." She thanked me a thousand times for changing her life around, but I reminded her that although I supported her through her journey, it was she who changed her own life.

Don't be afraid to create your own method for habit change. And never forget to pat yourself in the back for your accomplishment.

REMEMBER THE EASY HABIT WAY

There are four fundamental actions for creating or changing any habits. They are:

1. Change one habit at a time
2. Break it down to very small steps
3. Repeat, repeat, repeat
4. Reward yourself

CHAPTER SEVEN:

Habits of the Spirit

At the beginning of this book, I shared a spiritual experience that came to me when I was a very young child. I never thought about it as such, probably because the concept of spirituality was never discussed in my home. Later on in my life, throughout my nursing career, the focus was not on healing but on curing, not on the body/mind connection but on hard-core science and double-blind studies.

There was no room for spirituality in medicine until people like Dr. Larry Dossey, a physician and author of 12 books on the role of prayer and spiritualism in health care, revolutionized the concept of healing. Around the same time, another physician by the name of Bernie Siegel published a book called *Love, Medicine and Miracles*. Both of these pioneering physicians established a new paradigm in the field of medicine.

In my own personal experience as a critical care nurse, I have seen the power of spirituality unfold time and time again. Spiritually aware people displayed certain traits. They believed in a higher power, had faith in the goodness of the world and related a sense of connection to something bigger than themselves. They practiced self-reflection while searching for meaning in life, were described by friends and family as being kind and considerate, and preferred giving to taking. These men and women forgave others, were grateful, and smiled and laughed often. They showed empathy and compassion for the suffering of others and coped better with their own anguish. And sometimes they baffled the medical and nursing staff with unpredictable and miraculous outcomes. Most of the patients I have treated who lived by spiritual values were more at peace with themselves than those who did not.

If you are looking to develop a habit for a deeper spiritual connection, the tools are the same as for any other habit. You might want to start by cultivating your spirit with the practice of an energy-based movement such as Yoga or Tai Chi, or Qi Gong. You may prefer to start a meditation practice or join groups of like-minded people who share similar goals. Whatever you decide, schedule it in your calendar and repeat it on a regular basis until it becomes a part of your nature. Once you make it a habit of attending to the needs of your own soul, add something that you can do for others, perhaps an act of kindness every day. This could be just a smile to a stranger, opening a door for someone, giving food to the homeless, checking in on an older person, or calling someone to say hello.

THE HABIT OF PRAYER: A PERSONAL ACCOUNT

Shema, a six-word central element of a Jewish service, is the reminder that I've programmed on my iPhone. It is often thought of as a declaration of faith that Jews affirm and renew each day. It calls on the people of Israel to listen to the message of faith and is the introduction into Jewish prayer. For a long time, I'd pray once in a while when I remembered but I wanted to pray regularly. I wanted it to be a habit.

Raised in a Jewish home, all that I learned about my religion was what I observed from my parents. My father attended services regularly and, on the High Holy Days, my mother and I accompanied him. My mother lit the Sabbath candles and cooked traditional meals. That was the extent of her Jewish rituals. Instead of attending Hebrew School, I spent two years in a Catholic convent when we first arrived to Argentina in 1945. War brought on bizarre events in our lives. I did not like going to services on the High Holidays and was grateful not to have to go at other times. "Good thing you're a girl or you would have had to go more often," I would say to myself. I didn't understand anything about the service as it was all done in Hebrew and nothing was ever explained to me. It's not a surprise that I didn't grow up with a strong sense of religion. But I did grow up with a strong sense of spirituality. I'd been saved from the Holocaust and from very early on I sensed the presence of God.

Fast-forward many years to a grown woman with sons preparing for their Bar Mitzvah. Now I was drawn to learning more about Judaism. Today, I have my own prayer and I strive to learn the traditional psalms and prayers so I can sing and recite them along side my fellow congregants, one prayer at a time.

I keep the reminder on my phone even if I no longer need it since it has already become a habit. The prayer itself is not the habit. The habit is that I make it happen. The habit is that I focus on praising God, feeling gratitude for my blessings, and petition for peace and the healing of body, mind, and spirit for people who need it. The people I pray for and the words I use to connect with God may change from day to day, but the habit of praying is ingrained in my soul and it enriches my spirit.

Most religions recognize the power of regularity and rituals and ask us to develop habits of prayer and blessings. Fixed words and times for prayer are balanced with spontaneous and intentional prayer. Both are important.

Creating habits for a healthy spirit is no different than creating habits for a healthy body or mind. You need intention, awareness, a desire for that habit to be born and a call to action for change to occur. Habits of the spirit also require small and incremental changes and lots of repetition. When looking for someone to be accountable it's important to connect with a person who has the same values. Even better, work with someone who is looking to achieve the same goal.

CHAPTER EIGHT:

Habits for Children

When I was a little girl, my parents told me that as soon as I got home from school I had to change my clothes to either my play outfits or a *peignoir* (French for bathrobe). "This will save on the wear and tear of your good clothing," explained my father. Many years later I still do that quite automatically, even if I'm wearing my everyday jeans and I can afford the wear and tear on my 'good' clothes. It is a habit.

The habit of changing clothes when I got home spread to other good habits, such as hanging up what I was wearing as soon as I took them off and keeping my closet and desk neat and organized. The habit eventually helped me become an organized professional as well as a homemaker providing a pleasant and tidy environment for my family. Every one of these accomplishments was a small win that took me from one point to another. My parents, whether they knew it not, had taught me a keystone habit, a core habit that leads to the development of multiple other habits, like a chain reaction.

Most of the time, if we want to teach our children to grow up with good habits, all we need to do is set a good example by being role models and teaching them a few basic keystone habits. The rest will develop naturally because children are natural learners and do so all the time.

THE BROCCOLI-GOLDFISH STUDY

Professor Alison Gopnik is a developmental cognitive psychologist who has taken on the great challenge of exploring the minds of babies and young children. Together with colleague Betty Repacholi, PhD, they conducted studies to see how much babies understand the world around them, more specifically how they think and perceive the needs of others.

The experiment consisted of giving 14 and 18 month-old babies two bowls of food, one with raw broccoli and the other with Goldfish crackers. The babies tasted the food and made gestures that clearly indicated which food they did or did not like. Then, the researcher tasted the broccoli and made all kinds of faces and sounds to show how much she disliked it. But when she tasted the Goldfish crackers she did just the opposite. This took place for the first half of the experiment; for the other second half the researcher switched and made pleasant sounds and remarks about the broccoli and unpleasant ones about the Goldfish crackers. Then she extended her hand and asked them to give her some food. The results were quite interesting: the 18 month-old babies gave the researcher the broccoli where as the 14 month-old babies handed them the Goldfish crackers. The conclusion was that the 18-month-old babies had learned, in just a few months, to recognize someone else's perspective, giving them what they thought they wanted rather than what they would have chosen. [45]

Dr. Gopnik shows us in her studies that children, while exploring their environment through play and endless questions, are also hypothesizing, much like scientists do, to find answers and solutions to their questions. In an article entitled: "Your Baby Is Smarter Than You Think", Dr. Gopnik makes a powerful statement when she says: "But what children observe most closely, explore most obsessively and imagine most vividly are the people around them. There are no perfect toys; there is no magic formula. Parents and other caregivers teach young children by paying attention and interacting with them naturally and, most of all, by just allowing them to play." [46]

What these studies show is that children learn best in a safe environment where they are allowed to explore at their heart's content with some guidance from loving, supportive, and creative caregivers.

When it comes to teaching good habits to children, the crux is not so much how or what we should teach them but rather are WE ready to teach them? Do WE have habits that WE want our children to emulate? Do WE need to make some changes in our own habits?

❧

A PARENT'S ROLE

Ideally, every parent's wish is to raise their children to be fine citizens, good people who are independent, productive, honest, happy and healthy. How do we instill these habits early on?

Whether we teach them to brush their teeth, wash their hands after potty, say please and thank you, treat others with respect, say the truth, do their homework, or how to play and share with their friends, what we are really doing is instilling habits that will last them throughout their lives.

You might argue that having good manners, being truthful, sharing, and showing respect for others are values rather than habits, and you would be right. But remember, the definition of a habit is a behavior that we do almost automatically. Now, think about when you apply these values in your everyday life. Do you think about them or do you perform them almost automatically? When you hold a door for someone behind you, do you think about doing that or is the action automatic? When you are rushing through the subway and you accidentally bump into someone, do you have to think about saying "excuse me" or does it come naturally?

My six grandchildren, ranging from 26 to 11 years-old, all say "love you" when saying their good-byes. I know they love me, and I also know that "love you" has become the new farewell greeting. It has become a habit—and what a good one it is!!

DIFFERENT HABITS, DIFFERENT APPROACHES

Brushing teeth habits

Some habits, such as the habit of brushing your teeth, require two steps: the **how** and the **when**.

For example, Jane taught her daughter Tammy how to brush her teeth by giving her a baby toothbrush when she was two. At first, Jane just let her play with it. Later on she brought her to the bathroom and brushed her own teeth while Tammy watched and tried to imitate her. Eventually Tammy learned all the steps to brushing her teeth: pick up the toothbrush, squeeze the toothpaste on to it, get a glass of water, and brush, brush, brush. What she didn't learn was any set time to brush her teeth. Before she started school Tammy brushed her teeth sometime during the day when her mother would remind her. But once Tammy started school, since it wasn't a habit to brush her teeth at designated times, Tammy often went to school without brushing her teeth.

If you want your kids to brush their teeth at designated times, such as first thing in the morning, after meals, and before going to sleep then you have to keep after them until you see that they develop the habit and no longer need your reminders.

Sleeping habits

Since parents usually go to sleep after their kids, sleeping habits can't be learned by example. But they are extremely important to learn early on to set a healthy pattern throughout their lives. The transition between active daytime and getting ready for bed requires a routine that prepares the body, mind, and spirit for bedtime. Preparing clothing and school materials for the following day sets the mood that the day is about to end. Some of the guidelines provided by the National Sleep Foundation (see page 113) can be used with age appropriate modifications. Those include bedtime stories, a relaxing bath, a cozy time to talk about what they are grateful for or what the best part of their day was, prayers, mantras and anything else that fits into the routine. Not to worry; your kids won't grow up with the habit of having to be read a bedtime story (although it may be a precursor for the habit of reading in bed before sleep), and they will develop the habit of preparing for a good night's sleep.

Habits of mind and spirit

When children learn the habit of punctuality there's a good chance that they will learn about the concept of time. That gets translated to doing their homework on time, getting up early enough to make it to school in time and a host of other lessons that will benefit them throughout their lives. It's never too early to introduce children to their own calendars in which they can make notes of their activities. This is a wonderful way of introducing the "time" element and calculating together the amount of minutes or hours they would need to get ready to arrive at their destination on time.

Children get easily distracted because they are constantly taking in the world around them. Parental guidance to bring them back to focus will help mitigate procrastination.

There are many ways to teach children habits of gratitude. One way is through prayer and blessings before meals.

If you want your child to develop habits of generosity, kindness, and compassion provide them with something they can offer a homeless person or encourage them to be a part of a cause to help less fortunate people. Include them as much as possible in your own efforts to make this a better world. Take them to marches and walkathons and don't forget to make it FUN!

When it comes to teaching children good habits it helps to have an understanding of what will motivate them.

I recently had a discussion with a client about how to get her teenagers motivated to do chores around the house. My client felt that they should do their chores with no reward because that's what she asks them to do. "Just do it," she tells them, and if they don't they will be punished in some way (usually by removing one of their electronics or being grounded for a period of time). I asked her if that was working and the answer was no. I suggested that she change her ways and provide a reward for doing chores. We worked out a schedule of various chores and a fair monetary compensation and posted these for the teens so that they could sign up. The kids loved this new strategy. They found all kinds of work to do in the house, the yard, and with their pets. Mom was ecstatic.

Studies show that willpower is more easily recruited when people are highly motivated, be it by an extrinsic reward such as payment for work done or intrinsic reasons such as benefiting humanity. [47] Another strong motivator is when more explanations and respect is given rather than straightforward orders [48]. It's obvious why these teenagers responded so well to their new routine.

THE TRIPLE A'S WORK FOR ADOLESCENTS, TOO

Remember the Triple A's from Chapter Four? They work with teenagers as well as adults.

Alexa and her family are friends of mine. One day Alexa's father called her lazy. This upset the 17 year-old and, as a result, a family argument ensued. Alexa was defensive and argued against the label and her Dad apologized. Alexa accepted the apology and admitted that she did feel lazy many times, especially when it came to keeping her room tidy and doing her homework.

Awareness set in. Alexa decided she was going to make an effort to be more productive because she knew that her parents would reward her for her efforts as they had done in the past.

Motivation is very much at the core of laziness and it comes in a variety of forms. For Alexa, motivation came from a combination of defending herself against the lazy label (external/negative, because she was afraid of disapproval from her family) and the reward for changing her habit (internal/positive if the reward was pride in her accomplishments or external/positive if the reward was about something her parents would give her).

Alexa's **action** steps began by being intensely productive for 15 minutes in one area of her life once a week. She started with her room. She worked liked a demon for

15 minutes, straightening it out, hanging clothes and putting things in drawers. After 15 minutes she stopped. In addition, every night, just before going to sleep, she used the Mantra Habit as a subliminal suggestion. She tracked her progress using check marks on the calendar. Alexa found herself having fun during her intensely productive behavior with the game she had designed, following some of my suggestions. She enjoyed the challenge of how much she could accomplish before the 15 minutes were over.

Alexa also asked her kid brother, Paul, who was 9 years-old, to be her **accountability partner**. He looked up to his older sister and was very proud of being asked to fulfill the responsibility.

This was a win-win situation: Alexa changed her lazy habit and Paul learned that altering bad habits can be challenging but the journey could be made easier by reporting to an accountability partner. Gradually, Alexa added more days of the week and more hours to her high productive project until it became a good habit.

GOOD ROLE MODELS DISPLAY GOOD HABITS

Nothing beats being a good role model and creating a good example for your children to learn good habits. In

Chapter Five I talked about my patient Mary, whose posture was perfect to compensate for her scoliosis.

As a parent, it was a given that she would be a good posture role model for her kids. With a little gentle prodding she taught them how to sit properly when they did their homework, and she encouraged them to stretch often and try to stand more often than sit. She displayed pictures around the house to remind them of proper posture and bought them cervical pillows especially made for children. Although it's almost impossible to monitor sleeping position, especially with young children, parents can introduce the concepts of good sleeping posture before the kids go to sleep. This is the genesis of the subliminal Mantra Habit that can be introduced later on when the children are older and more able to understand the principles of good posture. Plus, improving posture is not only physically beneficial but it also has been proven that it can strengthen will power. [49]

Dr. Karen Erickson is a leading chiropractor based in New York City and the spokesperson for the American Chiropractic Association. She is emphatic about starting to teach children proper postural habits as early as possible, and in her large pediatric practice many of her patients are newborns. Dr. Erickson spends much of her time educating her patients, both adults and children, about the importance of proper posture for its beneficial effect on all organs of the body. She uses several methods, incorporating movements and postures, from Yoga and the Alexander Technique, to demonstrate proper posture. The Alexander Technique teaches awareness, changing deep unconscious postural habits.

Good posture isn't the only habit that can be taught. My friend Nan and her husband Jerry changed their own habits once they had kids. Eating dinner together as a family was a must in their household. They trained themselves to eat slower, chew their food well and be mindful at meal times. Here's a tip they shared about how they got their kids to chew their food well: they made it a game. Whoever could chew the longest got a prize. After a while, chewing thoroughly became a habit. The children also enjoyed naming the colors of the different fruits and vegetables while learning their nutritional value. The whole family drank water with their meals, and the kids learned that water was healthier than soda. When the kids got older they taught them the importance of reading labels on their packaged foods and explained the meaning of total calories, saturated fats, sugar and sodium.

Nan and Jerry took on a more active life themselves, and they exposed their children to a variety of physical activities until they found something that they enjoyed. They limited television viewing to less than one hour a day and encouraged reading, often taking them to the local bookstore so they could choose their own books. They urged them to spend time with friends and fostered an environment of self-esteem and positive mindset. Nan and Jerry knew that the best way to teach children manners and good habits was by being positive role models and by making learning fun.

THE NEED FOR HEALTHIER EATING HABITS

This is an area where teaching by example works best. Food shopping with your children is one way to teach about making healthy eating choices, provided of course that you, the parent, are well informed. I have often observed parents in the supermarket ask their young children if they wanted to buy certain foods. This is a great way to stimulate incentive for them to eat what they choose—as long as they are offered healthy choices.

My colleague Lindsay takes Lexi, her 3 year-old daughter, food shopping with her most of the time. "It takes me longer but it's well worth it," she says, "but sometimes it can be challenging. For instance, the other day Lexi picked up a box of chocolate chip cookies. She had seen her grandpa eating them and although she had never tasted one, she insisted on getting it." I was curious to find out how Lindsay handled the situation. Here's what she did: she told Lexi that Mommy didn't like those cookies because they had too much sugar and that wasn't good for her. (Lindsay asserted herself as the final decision maker.)

Then she went to the fruit department and bought grapes, which are Lexi's favorite fruit. Lexi was happy with that and soon forgot about the chocolate chip cookies.

"Does is always work out that way?" I asked. "Of course not," she responded, "but you try different strategies until something works."

Shopping with kids is also a great opportunity to make it an enjoyable age-appropriate lesson. When shopping with older kids it's invaluable to spend time reading labels, a habit that they will take with them throughout their lives.

Having as many family meals as possible helps children learn all aspects of healthy eating, which, as I described in previous chapters, goes beyond nutritious food and includes mindfulness and proper eating manners.

My friend Angela Marie Franco is the author of *The Table Manners Coach*. But manners and etiquette is not her only focus of interest; Angela also teaches children ages 4-11 how to cook nutritious meals using fresh ingredients without the use of a stove, a microwave, or any other heating element. While having fun creating their own recipes, these kids also learn to make nutritious choices - a habit of health that could very well become a keystone for many other good habits. [50]

While it is not possible to put a value on which habit is more important for kids to learn, we cannot ignore the obesity crisis that has spilled over to our children. One in three children is overweight or obese. According to the CDC, since 1980 obesity in children has more than doubled, and in adolescents it has more than quadrupled, in the U.S. A diagnosis of adult onset diabetes is now known as Type 2 in order to include the pediatric and adolescent population. Studies show that overweight kids are likely to become overweight and obese adults. In a recent issue of the *New York Times* Jane Brody discusses the rise in blood pressure seen in obese children. [51]

Healthy eating habits, as well as other habits, are learned early in childhood. In addition to curbing consumption of sugary sweetened drinks, avoiding calorie-dense foods, and providing nutritious meals and snacks, parents need to model good eating habits beyond food. Providing plenty of time to eat in a pleasant environment where children are free to express themselves is paramount in ensuring a proper foundation for healthy eating. Creating new habits is much easier than changing bad ones. Children don't come into the world with bad habits. It's up to us to start them off learning good habits.

WHERE DO YOU BEGIN?

Being aware of your own unhealthy habits, and taking action steps to change them, is a good place to start. In this book I've outlined the best practices for changing un-healthy habits and creating optimal health going forward. These guidelines are for adults. Children just require gentle direction, opportunities to discover the world around them, good role models, a few age-appropriate modifications and a creative and enjoyable approach to learning good habits.

But adopting healthy habits should start a long time before children arrive. An article in the *New York Times* discusses a study that traces the origins of being overweight and obese even before the mother's pregnancy. It included the father's weight as well because "being heavy alters DNA in the father's sperm that changes gene expression and can be passed down to the next generation." It looks like pre-nuptial preparations should include a healthy weight of both partners if they are planning a family. (52)

PUTTING IT ALL TOGETHER

"When we look at living creatures from an outward point of view, one of the first things that strike us is that they are bundles of habits." This is the opening sentence in Chapter IV of William James's book *The Principles of Psychology*. (53) The chapter is named "Habits." The book was written in 1890.

Williams stressed the urgency of forming good habits early on and proposed that the personality of humans may be a direct compilation of habits. He stated: "Could the young but realize how soon they will become mere walking bundles of habits, they would give more heed to their conduct while in the plastic state."

To this I would add that the role of parents in shaping the character of their children rests on the values and the habits that they pass on to them.

Final Words

We are body, mind, and spirit. When the three are in unison we can achieve our goals quicker and more effectively. Much like the legs of a stool, the three work in tandem for balancing our outward behavior.

There are various methods and approaches to changing our habits. Each of us has to find the method that best reflects his/her body, mind, and spirit. Some prefer to do it on their own while others may prefer to have assistance of a coach. There is no right or wrong way. There is only the way that is right for YOU!

I invite you to share with me your experiences about creating and/or changing habits whether you have used any of the techniques mentioned in this book or with one of your own methods. My email is <u>drsylvie@healthyhabitsdoctor.com.</u> (I will reply to your email.) I look forward to hearing your story and what has worked for you. I am ready to serve as your accountability partner any time.

It is my deepest wish that this book will motivate you to be free of habits that are pulling you down. You owe it yourself, and the world around you, to express everything you can be in body, mind, and spirit.

"Watch your thoughts, for they become words.
Choose your words, for they become actions.
Understand your actions, for they become habits.
Study your habits, for they become your character.
Develop your character, for it becomes your destiny."

–Frank Outlaw

Sources

1. Wayne Scott Andersen, *Dr. A's Habits of Health: The Path To Permanent Weight Control And Optimal Health* (Annapolis: Habits of Health Press, 2008).

2. Neal, D.,Wood, W., Wu, M., Kurlander, D., "The Pull Of The Past." *Pers Soc Psychology Bull.* 2011; Vol. 37 no.11 1428-1437.

3. Conversation with Robert Dally, PhD., October 2008.

4. Koch, C. *Change Management: Understanding the Science of Change.* CIO publication - CXO Media Inc. (a subsidiary of IDG Enterprise. 2016; September 15, 2016.

5. Smith, K., Virkud, A., Deisseroth, K., Graybiel, A. "Reversible online control of habitual behavior by optogenic pertubation of medial prefrontal cortex." *Proceedings of the National Academy of Sciences.* 2012; Vol. 109 no. 46 18932-18937.

6. Old, J., Milner, P. "Positive Reinforcement Produced by Electrical Stimulation of Septal Area and Other Regions of Rat Brain." *Journal of Comparative Physiological Psychology.* 1954; Vol. 47 419-27.

7. Mischel, W., Ebbesen, E. "Cognitive and attentional mechanisms in delay gratification." *Journal of Personality and Social Psychology.* 1972; Vol. 21 no. 2 204-18.

8. Baumeister, R., Bratslavsky, E., Muraven, M., Tice, D. Ego Depletion: Is the Active Self a Limited Resource? *Journal of Personality and Social Psychology.* 1998; Vol. 74 no.5 1252-1265.

9. Jenkins, D. J., Wolever, TM., Vurksan, V., Brighenti, F., Cunnane, SC., Rao, AV., Jenkins, AL., Buckley, G., Patten, R., Singer, W., et al. "Nibbling versus Gorging: metabolic advantages of increased meal frequencies." *New England Journal of Medicine.* 1989; 321 (14): 929-34.

10. Roy Baumeister and John Tierney, *Willpower: Rediscovering the Greatest Human Strength.* (New York: Penguin Publishing Group, 2011).

11. Molden, D.C., Hui, C.M., Scholer, A.A., Meier, B.P., Noreen, E.E., D'Agostino, P.R., Martin, V. "Motivational

Versus Metabolic Effects of Carbohydrates on Self Control." *Psychological Science.* 2012; Vol 23 no. 10 1137 to 1144.

12. Baumeister, R.F., Gailliot, M., DeWall, C.N., Oaten, M. "Self-Regulation and Personality: How Interventions Increase Regulatory Success and How Depletion Moderates the Effects of Traits on Behavior." *Journal of Personality.* 2006; Vol 74 Issue 6 1773-1802.

13. Muraven, M. "Mechanisms of Self-Control Failure: Motivation and Limited Resources." *Personality and Social Psychology Bulletin,* 2003; Vol. 29 no.7 894-906.

14. Oaten, M., Ching, K. "Longitudinal gains in self-regulation from regular physical exercise." *British Journal Health Psychology.* 2006; Vol. 11 PT 4: 717-33.

15. Brandon Buchard, (2014) *The Motivation Manifesto: 9 Declarations to Claim Your Personal Power* (Carlsbad, New York City, London, Sydney, Johannesburg, Vancouver, Hong Kong, New Delhi: Hay House, Inc., 2014).

16. M. Scott Peck, *The Road Less Traveled: A New Psychology of Love, Traditional values and Spiritual Growth* (New York: Simon & Schuster, 1978).

17. Graham, S., Weiner, B. "Drive-Reduction Theory of Motivation." *Boundless Psychology.* 2016; *Retrieved 01 Oct. 2016 from https://www.boundless.com/psychology/textbooks/boundless-psychology-textbook/motivation-12/theories-of-motivation-65/drive-reduction-theory-of-motivation-250-12785.*

18. Yerkes, R.M., Dodson, J.D. "The Relation of Strength of Stimulus to Rapidity of Habit Formation." *Journal of Comparative Neurology and Psychology.* 1908; Vol. 18 459-482.

19. Lunenburg, F.C. "Expectancy Theory of Motivation: Motivating by Altering Expectations." *International Journal of Management, Business, and Administration.* 2011; Vol 15 no 1.

20. Maslow, A.H. "A Theory of Human Motivation." *Psychological Review.* 1943; Vol. 50 no 4 370-396.

21. James O. Prochaska, John C. Norcross, and, Carlo C. DiClemente, *Changing For Good: A Revolutionary Six-Stage Program For Overcoming Bad Habits and Moving Your Life Positively Forward* (New York: Harper Collins Publishers, 1994).

22. Fogg, B.J. (2013) TED x Fremont

23. Caroline I. Arnold, *small move, big change* (New York: Penguin Group, 2014).

24. Charles Duhigg, The Power of Habit: *Why We Do What We Do In Life and Business* (New York: Random House, 2014).

25. Art Markman, *Smart Change: Five Tools To Create New And Sustainable Habits In Yourself and Others* (New York: Penguin Group, 2014).

26. Dave Sellars, *Stop or Start Habits with Outcome Visioning TM* (Grand Rapids: FutureSelfInstitute LLC. 2016).

27. Amy Johnson, (2016) *The Little Book of Change: The No-Willpower Approach To Breaking Any Habit* (Oakland, CA: New Harbinger Publications, Inc., 2016).

28. Chopra, D. Meditation series: Getting Unstuck. (2016).

29. Maxwell Maltz, *Psycho-Cybernetics* (New York: Simon & Schuster, 1960).

30. Lally, P., Van Jaarsveld, C.H.H., Potts, H.W.W., Wardle, J. "How are habits formed: Modelling habit formation in the real world." *European Journal of Social Psychology.* 2009; Vol 40 issue 6 998-1009.

31. Winfrey, O. Meditation Series: Getting Unstuck. (2016).

32. Roni Caryn Rabin, "Worried You're Not Alone", *New York Times* Well Section, May 9, 2016.

33. Jennifer Jolly, "A Shocking Way (Really) to Break Habits", *New York Times* Well Section, May 2, 2016.

34. Woolf, S.H., Laudan, A. "U.S. Health in International Perspectives: Shorter Lives, Poorer Health." Institute of Medicine of the National Academies. Washington, DC, 2013.

35. Press Release: "1 in 3 adults don't get enough sleep." CDC Newsroom Centers for Disease Control and Prevention. (Atlanta: 2016).

36. Gangwisch, J.E., Heymsfield, B., Boden-Abda, B., Buijs, R.M., Kreler, F., Pickering, T.G., Rundle, A.G., Zammit, G.K., Malaspina, D. "Short Sleep Duration as a Risk Factor for Hypertension." *Hypertension*. 2006; Vol. 47, Issue 5.

37. Barone, M.T.U., Menna-Barreto, L. "Diabetes and Sleep: A complex cause-and-effect relationship." *Diabetes Research and Clinical Practice*. 2011: Vol 91 Issue 2 129-137.

38. Capuccio, F.P., Cooper, D., D'Elia, L., Strazzulo, P., Miller, M.A. "Sleep duration predicts cardiovascular outcomes: a systematic review meta-analysis of prospective studies." *European Heart Journal.* 2011: Vol 32 Issue 12 1484-1492.

39. National Sleep Foundation poster. Reprinted with permission.

40. Jason M. Satterfield, J.M., *Mind-Body Medicine: The New Science of Optimal Health* (Chantily, Virginia: The Great Courses, 2013).

41. Wayne Scott Andersen, *Discover Your Optimal Health: The Guide to Taking Control of Your Weight, Your Vitality, Your Life* (Boston: Da Capo Press, 2013).

42. Wendy Hendry, *W.A.I.T. loss: The Keys to Food Freedom and Winning the Battle of the Binge* (Riverton: Bookwise Publishers, 2015).

43. Sandra Aamodt, "Why you can't lose weight on a diet". *New York Times, Well Section* May 6, 2016.

44. Gina Kolata, "Many Weight-Loss Ideas Are Myth, Not Science, Study Finds", *New York Times, National,* January 31, 2013.

45. Rapacholi, B.M., Gopnik, A. "Early reasoning about desires: Evidence from 14-and 18-month olds." *Developmental Psychology.* 1997: Vol 33 no 1 12-21.

46. Alison Gopnik, "Your Baby Is Smarter Than You Think", *New York Times The Opinion Page*, August 15, 2009.

47. Muraven, M., Gagne, M, Rosman, H. "Helpful Self-Control: Autonomy Support, Vitality, and Depletion." *Journal of Experimental Psychology.* 2008: Vol 44 no. 3 573-585.

48. Muraven, M. "Mechanisms of Self-Control Failure: Motivation and Limited Resources." *Pers. Soc. Psychol. Bulletin.* 2003: Vol. 29 no. 7 894-906.

49. Noel, R. *The Journal of Positive Psychology.* 2012: Vol 7 No 5 446-448 Book Review: *Willpower: Rediscovering the greatest human strength* by Roy F. Baumeister and John Tierney. New York: Penguin Press, 2011.)

50. Angela Marie Franco, *The Table Manners Coach: A Lifestyle Perspective for Comfort and Poise in Any Dining Situation* (New York: AMF Direct LLC, 2004).

51. Jane Brody, "High Blood Pressure in Children", *New York Times* Well Section, September 12, 2016.

52. Jane Brody, "To Stem Obesity, Start Before Birth", *New York Times,* Well Section, July 11, 2016.

53. William James, (1890) *The Principles of Psychology: Chapter IV Habit* with Introduction by George A. Miller (Boston: Harvard University Press, 1983).